CW00825769

TOWARDS THE
WICCAN CIRCLE

Sorita d'Este

*Selfstudy manual based on the
Successful homestudy course*

Published by Avalonia

BM Avalonia
London
WC1N 3XX
England, UK

www.avaloniabooks.co.uk

TOWARDS THE WICCAN CIRCLE

ISBN (10) 1-905297-05-X
ISBN (13) 978-1-905297-05-4

First Edition, SEPTEMBER 2008
Based on the material from the Avalonia *"Towards the Wiccan Circle"* homestudy Course © 2005.
Copyright © 2008 Sorita d'Este, Avalonia

Illustrations by Satori
Design by Satori

Cover Illustration by Emily Carding
© Emily Carding, www.childofavalon.com

TOWARDS THE
WICCAN CIRCLE

Sorita d'Este

a practical introduction
to the principles of Wicca

INTRODUCTION

Towards the Wiccan Circle was originally designed as a homestudy course to introduce individuals interested in exploring the Wiccan tradition to the key principles and practices of the tradition. It was based on the practical Introduction to Wicca courses David Rankine and I facilitated in London for a number of years, with each lesson introducing a new concept and building on the knowledge gained in the previous. In addition to the *Towards the Wiccan Circle* homestudy course we also offered the *Avalonia Wicca Course* (2002-2006) which was a more comprehensive course that also explored a number of natural magick practices. Due to personal commitments it became impossible for us to continue offering these courses and in late 2007 we made the decision to no longer take new students on.

During the time we offered the courses we had several hundred students from around the world working through with personal support from David and myself. Students from as far apart as Korea, Australia, South Africa, Mexico, Chile, Brazil, China, Scotland, Germany, England, Italy, Wales, Sweden, Canada and the United States all successfully completed the courses. Many students became personal friends and we have probably learned as much from them as they have from us!

The courses were created in the spirit of providing reliable and affordable supported training for people who were otherwise unable to find a teacher in their local area, or who because of personal circumstances were unable to commit to such training. Many of the courses which were being offered at the time were extraordinarily expensive, which was not in the spirit of the tradition I was taught in myself.

After closing the course to new students in 2007 we continued to get a steady stream of inquiries about it. Initially we had no plans on publishing the material as we felt there were enough *"beginners"* books on the subject of Wicca and Pagan Witchcraft available already. However, as time went by it became apparent that through word of mouth people were interested in doing this course in particular, so we decided to adapt it for publication in 2008. Of course the support offered by a mentor cannot be expressed in a book in the same way it can through interaction and exchanges of correspondence, but I tried to incorporate as many of the ideas and questions which students asked during the course of the years the course was offered into the material in this manual. The original course had feedback questions and knowledge tests for students to complete, in this course much of this has been replaced by additional practical exercises.

It is important to keep in mind that this course is not representative of any one particular tradition of Wicca or Pagan Witchcraft. Instead it was designed it to represent the ideas which are held in common within a number of established traditions today. This self-study course manual is intended as a starting point for further studies into the mysteries of the Craft and the Art Magickal.

Sometimes key principles are taken for granted by those with plenty of experience, which may leave beginners confused and worse, misdirected. Whilst naturally *"mystery"* plays an important role in all magickal traditions, there are some things that can be made much easier with a little bit of guidance and a nudge in the right direction, leaving time and energy – as well as providing motivation – for exploring the deeper mysteries!

I hope that you will enjoy working through this manual and that it will provide insights for you into the Wiccan tradition which will help you find you own unique path – whichever direction that might take, I sincerely hope that it is as unique as you are!

Blessings
Sorita d'Este
Monmouthshire, Wales

USING THIS GUIDE

As with all things magickal it is entirely up to you how you approach and use the material presented in this book, however by following these simple guidelines you will ensure that you get the best out of this self-study guide:

⊕ You will need a suitable notebook for use as a magickal diary in which you will keep notes as you progress through this course of study. See Appendix 2 for ideas and suggestions on how to keep your magickal diary.

⊕ Approach the material lesson by lesson, starting with lesson 1:

o First read through the entire lesson;

o Then re-read the material and complete each exercise to the best of your ability;

o Make sure to take your time, there is no hurry. The original course was designed to be completed in six to twelve months.

o Be patient with yourself. Some of the exercises (especially the visualisation ones) might seem really simple at first, but they can take time to master, so again take your time and don't be hard on yourself if it takes you longer than you thought.

⊕ When you have completed all the lessons in the book, remember that many of the exercises can be used again and again, so make sure to copy them into your magickal journal if you found them useful so that you have them to hand for future use.

Additional material by the same authors can be found at www.avalonia.co.uk – including many free articles which might be useful to you.

CONTENTS

LESSON 1

PAGANISM, WITCHCRAFT & WICCA

"You wear the robes of the old, old gods"[1]

The magickal world is a confusing one, full of strange words, sometimes with multiple meanings. As many magickal traditions were oral traditions for centuries, before being written down, there are sometimes many difficulties in trying to establish the correct use of a word. To make matters even more complicated, the meanings of many words have also changed with the passing of time and sometimes they have come to mean different things, to different people. Add to that the fact that the world of magick and witchcraft is generally a secretive one and it becomes no surprise that sometimes things are wrongly interpreted from time to time.

Many newcomers to the world of modern Paganism are faced with the dilemma of what to call themselves, when they are not yet sure which path they wish to take. It can get extremely confusing when there are now so many different traditions, all offering something slightly different. For this reason our advice to newcomers is to describe themselves as someone who is *'interested in...'* whichever tradition they are exploring, rather than as practitioners of anything. This both avoids misunderstandings and also avoids a situation where you label yourself as being part of a tradition that you may find out in time is not the right one for you. At the end of the day, we are all many different things and applying labels can become restrictive. There is so much out there to explore, so look at a variety of traditions and paths before deciding which is right for you!

[1] Inanna and Ebih – High Priestess Enheduanna, 2300 BCE

Defining Wicca

It is likely that you already have some preconceived ideas of what *'Wicca'* means; on the other hand you may not. What is certain is that the question *"What is Wicca?"* surfaces on a very regular basis and that even within the Wiccan community definitions usually vary considerably and are the subject of much debate. To start with here are a few statements which may seem contradictory at first, but are all true:

★ All Wiccans are Witches;
★ Witches are not all Wiccan;
★ Witches are not all Pagan;
★ Pagans are not all Wiccan.

In order to clarify these statements, we need to now first examine what the terms *'Paganism'* and *'Witchcraft'* are taken to mean from a universal viewpoint:

Paganism

Paganism is an umbrella term used today to describe a wide range of practices, not a single belief system. The traditions that may fall under this term originate out of a range of many systems from a variety of cultural and geographical origins. When we use the term we use it to describe all the different modern Pagan religions and traditions. Many of the modern traditions are reconstructionist in their approach to their practices and beliefs, drawing from historical sources or in some instances, merging different ancient practices to create a new synthesis that is relevant to the world we live in today. Pagans today include henotheists, polytheists, pantheists, monotheists and a number of other –theists. Not all Pagans acknowledge a Goddess or a God, as some work with other natural forces instead, and some with Gods, Goddesses, Nature Spirits and a number of other Spiritual creatures.

The Latin noun *'Paganus'* was used by the Romans to refer to a country dweller or someone from the smaller villages outside of the cities and towns of the ancient world. It was not originally used as a word for a spiritual tradition, but rather to refer to someone in a derogatory way, implying that they were not as civilised or educated as those in the cities. With the increasing power of the Christian faith, those in the cities were usually the first to be converted to the new religion of Christianity, whilst those living in the countryside held onto their older beliefs and practices for longer. As a result the term *Paganus* became synonymous with those who followed a spiritual / religious path other than that of Christianity or one of the other *'Abrahamic'* religions, but who instead clung to the beliefs and practices of their ancestors.

The upsurge in interest in the Classical Pagan Myths during the Victorian Era, made way for the rebirth of a new Pagan movement, who would reclaim the term *'Pagan'* as their own, regardless of its original usage. Interestingly a high percentage of modern *'Pagans'* live in cities, rather than in the countryside, so the word is no longer taken to mean someone who is necessarily uneducated or who lives in the countryside! In fact many who use the term for themselves are professionals – including many academics and scholars.

Witchcraft

Another important distinction which you need to make from the beginning is that although the terms *'Witchcraft'* and *'Wicca'* have long been used interchangeably, they don't mean exactly the same thing. Witchcraft is used to describe a number of different practices from all around the world and although it's popular use amongst modern Pagans may seem to indicate that all Witches are also Pagan, this is not entirely true.

"A Hebrew Witch, a Pagan Witch, a Lapland Witch, an Indian Witch, a Protestant Witch, and a Popish Witch, are different from one another; some in Honour, and some in Disgrace."[2]

Practitioners of Witchcraft in a global sense may follow any number of spiritual paths and some even claim to be atheists. Long before the Christian Church villainised those who practiced the Old Religions, the term was being used to describe those who used the magickal arts for negative and malignant ends. Witches were despised even by the Priesthoods of the pre-Christian Pagan Gods – in Greece, Rome, Egypt and all over the ancient world. But for one reason or

---

[2] An Historical Essay Concerning Witchcraft, Hutchinson, 1718.

another it is the term that became used by people like Margaret Murray and subsequently Gerald Gardner, for both many of the practices now associated with the modern Pagan movement, as well as for the spiritual beliefs related with it.

The term has taken on a modern meaning, which although historically imprecise, has meaning to those using it today. Due to the confusion the term may cause and to distinguish themselves from those with other spiritual practices, many Witches who have Pagan spiritual beliefs, but who may not share in the same beliefs or practices as Wiccans, use the term *'Pagan Witch'* to describe themselves, whilst others prefer to simply use the term *'Witch'*. This is ultimately a personal choice. If you practice Witchcraft, you are a Witch after all!

Although Wicca contains aspects of what may be considered Witchcraft, it also contains a number of other elements – such as for example the celebration of the seasonal Sabbats, a Goddess and a God and healing. Wicca also draws from classical Paganism (in particular that of Rome and Greece) and the Western Mystery Tradition (including from Ceremonial Magick, Qabalah and Hermetic sources).

Exercise 1.1 - Your Definitions

Define for yourself the terms Wicca, Witchcraft and Paganism.
What are the significant differences between them?
Which of these terms do you feel applies to your path?
Now try to define Wicca again, seeing if your definition changes at all, and think how you would explain it to somebody who had never heard of it. Write this definition into your magickal diary, so that you have a reference point to look back on in the future as your perspective changes through experience.

THE WICCAN TRADITION

Trying to define Wicca in a few words on paper is not an easy task as it is essentially an oral and experiential tradition. In terms of traditional Gardnerian or Alexandrian Wicca (or initiatory traditions derived from them), Wicca is an Initiatory Mystery Tradition in which an initiate learns, by experience, from other members in the coven and in particular from the High Priestess and/or High Priest, about the rituals and practices of the tradition.

In this context initiation serves as a symbolic death and rebirth, as the postulant is reborn as a member of the tradition through the ceremony of First Degree Initiation, after which they take a different name (witch name) which is subsequently only used in ceremonies with other initiates in their coven.

Some of the more recent traditions, especially those which adapted the rituals for solitary use, advocate the use of a solitary self-dedication rite to mark the point at which the person is ready to undertake a lifelong commitment towards the Gods. Though this is of course a valid practice, it is important here to distinguish between a dedication to the Gods and initiation into a coven. Both are important steps in magickal development and both are important commitments, but they are not the same and for the sake of clarity it is important to have a clear understanding of what they entail before embarking on either and we will explore this in more depth in Lesson 7 – *"Initiation & Rites of Passage"*.

Wicca is an experiential Mystery Tradition. It can only be fully understood through experience. The key rituals, beliefs, practices and philosophies of the tradition can be summarised as being composed of three key component parts:

★ Magick
★ Mysticism
★ Spirituality

Magick has been famously described, as *"the art and science of causing change to occur in conformity with will"* by the Victorian magickian Aleister Crowley and it is also an apt description for how magick is used within Wicca. Magick can be seen as the directed interaction of the techniques used to make changes happen and produce the goals you were aiming for. In Wicca this is expressed through the working of spells (results magick), healing, the creation of charms (talismans & amulets) and through its use for personal empowerment and development.

Mysticism, from a Wiccan perspective, is experienced through the rites of initiations and other ceremonies that help to create a different state of consciousness. Initiations provide a shared experience within a particular tradition and the groups which are related to it, and first degree initiation also contains an element of symbolic rebirth as a member of the tradition and a welcoming into the coven, as well as alignment to the magickal current of the tradition. Mysticism is also experienced through the attainment of direct knowledge of the Gods and Goddesses who a Wiccan may work with, for which a number of techniques are used.

Spirituality is self-evident in Wicca through the celebration of the Gods and Goddesses through the natural cycles of the year – both in the seasons (Wheel of the Year) and the Moon (Lunar or Esbat workings). It is further expressed in covens through the ceremonies of Drawing Down the Moon and Drawing Down the Sun and when performing personal devotional workings. Spirituality is also expressed through the ethics of the tradition, as a radiation of the natural and holistic worldview which is developed through a focus on natural harmony and balance.

The best way of learning about the tradition is still through working with, and receiving initiation into a reputable coven. In this traditional way you are taught by a High Priest or High Priestess, who was taught in the same way by their High Priest or Priestess, who was also taught in this manner. In this way knowledge is passed from one to another, but together with knowledge the combined experience of those in the same line of initiation is also passed on to the next generation, who then receive its cumulative benefits and may in turn pass it on to their own initiates in due course adding to it insights gained through their own experience.

Though much has been written and published about the practices of the tradition, there are still parts of it that are best taught through practice, emphasising the need for an experiential component in gaining an understanding of the tradition.

Though the tradition continues to be taught in the traditional way today, there are also many more people who want to explore the practices and beliefs of Wicca who for one reason or another are unable to join a coven. These people often use the term 'Solitary' to describe themselves and use published materials as the basis for their work, teaching themselves about the tradition's beliefs and exploring its practices in solitary workings. These self-taught practitioners may also work with others where public ceremonies and workshops are available, or through forming study groups with others who share the same interests. Some even form their own covens when they have gained sufficient experience and knowledge.

There are still some who argue that the only way that you can claim membership of the tradition is through initiation into the tradition. However it is important to keep an open mind as it is certainly possible to practice many of the component parts of the tradition today by using published texts and to gain a good understanding thereof through experience, without having received initiation. If it is the practice of 'Wicca' that makes you a Wiccan, then it can be argued that those who work from published materials to establish their own way of working might indeed be practising Wicca, therefore they are then also logically Wiccan! There are differences though and these will be further explored in Lesson 7.

Wiccans honour both the divine feminine and divine masculine, expressed as the Goddess and God, who are viewed as the Moon Goddess and the Horned God. It emphasises growth through balance and discipline, which in turn brings about changes in perception regarding to the world we live in. Balance is expressed through the focus on polarity through which a dynamic tension is created, symbolically this is sometimes seen as the union of Goddess and God, but also through light and dark, active and passive and the magickal axiom of *"As Above, So Below"*.

The celebration of the Gods is at the heart of Wicca. Goddesses celebrated in Wicca are often associated with the Moon, but may also be stellar, terrestrial and chthonian. The patron God of Wicca is associated with forests, plants and animals. We often call him the Horned One, or Cernunnos, but sometimes we also work with Solar and chthonian Gods.

Exercise 1.2 - Experiences of the Path

Magick, Mysticism and Spirituality – what do these concepts mean to you, and how important are they. Does one stand out more at this time? Do you feel you have had experiences which characterise each of these concepts, and if so what were they? Record any experiences that have really stood out for you in your magickal diary.

WHAT DO WICCANS BELIEVE?

Wiccans celebrate the divine as both male and female, God and Goddess. However, the way in which the divine is viewed is left to the individual and will be based on their own experiences, personal work and soul searching. Wiccans are usually polytheistic, pantheistic, panentheistic or henotheistic. Many believe that all Goddesses are manifestations of the original feminine divine and that all Gods are likewise manifestations of the original masculine divine. A good example of how this is expressed in Wicca can be found in the opening lines of the *Charge of the Goddess*: *"Listen to the words of the Great Mother; she who of old was also called among men Artemis, Astarte, Athene, Dione, Melusine, Aphrodite, Ceridwen, Dana, Arianrhod, Isis, Bride, and by many other names..."*

Some traditions of Wicca also have special patron deities, thus members of a particular tradition or Coven may work with a particular God and Goddess. These names are sometimes kept oathbound, which means that they are not divulged outside of the tradition, though some groups do not subscribe to this practice. Traditionally Goddesses such as Diana, Aradia, Hekate, Artemis, Ceridwen and Arianrhod are favoured by Wiccans. They are all lunar goddesses, sometimes also with stellar associations. Gods such as Cernunnos, Pan and Herne are favoured, all sharing a strong association with the natural landscape, forests and all of whom are also of course depicted with horns. The beliefs of Wiccans are explored in more depth in Lesson 3 - *"The Gods & Goddesses"*.

Wiccan Sabbats

Followers of the Wiccan Tradition all celebrate the changing seasons in ceremonies that mark particular points in the year. There are eight seasonal festivals, divided into two groups, these are:

The Greater Sabbats
★ Samhain (All Hallows) – 31st October
★ Imbolc (Bride) – 1st February
★ Beltane (Roodmas) – 1st May
★ Lughnasadh (Lammas) - 1st August

The Lesser Sabbats
★ Winter Solstice (Yule) – approx. 21st December
★ Spring Equinox (Ostara or Eostre) – approx. 22nd March
★ Summer Solstice (Litha) – approx. 21st of June
★ Autumn Equinox (Modron) – approx. 21st of September

The Greater Sabbats are, according to Wiccan lore, the original festivals celebrated by Wiccans; they mark agricultural points in the year. We know these were celebrated in the past, as the ninth century Irish text, the *Psalter of Cashel*, records details of the druids celebrating these four festivals with great fires. This is entirely in keeping with these Sabbats being called the *'fire festivals'*.

The Lesser Sabbats were believed to have been celebrated in the past by the Druids. Certainly the Druids of recent centuries who revived what they knew of the old practices, focused on the Solar year, marking the journey of the Sun through the heavens with these festivals. They were incorporated into Wiccan practices during the late 1950's. The Lesser Sabbat dates are fixed as they are determined by the actual days on which either the Solstice or Equinox for that particular year falls on. Thus the shortest night will always be Midsummer, and the longest night always Midwinter.

For this reason the Equinoxes and Solstices should be celebrated on the exact date of the event, whenever possible. The Greater Sabbats may be celebrated on or near to the dates on which they traditionally fall. Some prefer to hold them on the Full Moon nearest the traditional date, others on days when there are particular omens from nature indicating that it is time for that festival. So for instance, some wait for the first snowdrops to bloom as a sign that it is time to celebrate Imbolc, likewise for the first hawthorn blossoms to appear as a sign that Beltane should be celebrated.

The celebration of the Sabbat rituals is central to Wiccan practice, in particular those of the Greater Sabbats, which are always marked with a ceremony.

The term *"Sabbat"* is derived from the Hebrew word *Shabat*, meaning *"to cease, rest"*, which itself is derived from the word *Shabbatai*, meaning *Saturn*, and referring to Saturday as the seventh day of creation. In medieval times witches were thought to meet on the Sabbath, and this term later became changed to Sabbat and used to describe the festivals.

Wiccan Esbats

In addition to the Wheel of the Year celebrations, some covens and solitaries also hold rituals at the Full Moon and other lunar phases. These ceremonies are commonly known as Esbats and are often centred on results magick such as healing, as well as devotional workings. In covens Esbats are usually exclusively for initiates of the coven, whereas trainees (also called dedicants, neophytes or probationers) are often included for the Sabbat celebrations. Esbats may be held at each of the Full Moons, or on an *"as needed"* basis. The term *"Esbat"* is thought to derive from the French word *s'esbattre* meaning *"to frolic"*.

WICCAN CEREMONY

From a traditional perspective Wiccan ceremonies are only performed by initiates of the tradition working with their coven. Over the last few decades, with a significant increase in the amount of information available, more people than ever before are using material from published sources to create their own 'Wiccan Style' ceremonies with which they celebrate the Divine Feminine and Divine Masculine, as well as the changing seasons.

Although there are still many differences between the practices of those working by themselves, from published material, and those who are able to work and receive initiation into a coven, the key elements of the ceremonies used are usually quite similar. The same can be said about the different groups and traditions within Wicca today, they may have different flavours, they may indeed use different words and they may even call on different deities, but they key elements of the ceremonies usually contain all or nearly all of the following component parts:

Ceremonial Opening:

★ Purification of the Ritual Space

This is usually done through the blessing of Salt & Water, with which the space which the ceremony will be performed is sprinkled. It may additionally include censing with incense.

★ Purification / Blessing of the Participants

This is usually done through anointing with oil or water (which has been consecrated) on the forehead. There are a number of other methods which may be used instead.

★ Casting the Circle

In a group (coven) this is usually done by the High Priestess, the High Priest or the coven Maiden. The appointed person speaks words of intent as they mark the circle with a sword, athame or wand. Solitary practitioners usually use their dominant hand for the purpose, whilst some use a wand or athame.

★ Invocation of the Guardians of the Four Cardinal Points

In a group this may be done by four appointed persons, one per direction/Element. Those working alone will do all four the elements themselves. Each Guardian is invoked at their appropriate place in the circle. It is also sometimes called the invocation of the Lords of the Watchtowers or the invocation of the Guardians of the Four Elements.

★   Invocation of the Deities (Goddess and God)

This is usually done by the High Priestess and High Priest in covens. Solitaries usually ask for the blessings of the Gods they are working with on their ritual. It is usual in some traditions to also invoke the Old Ones at this point in the ceremony, usually before the Gods are invoked.

★   Magickal workings

After the Gods have been invoked, it is time to perform any celebrations, games, dances, spells and any other magickal workings. This can be described as the *'purpose'* of the ceremony.

★   Cakes & Wine

After all magickal work has been completed, it is time to honour the feminine and masculine divine through the symbolic union of opposites in the ceremony of cakes and wine. This is usually performed by the High Priestess and High Priest in coven ceremonies. Solitaries will usually ask for the blessings of their deities on the cakes and wine

★   Rite of departure for the God

This is done as a farewell and thanksgiving to the masculine divine at the end of the ceremony.

★   Rite of departure for the Goddess

This is done as a farewell and thanksgiving to the feminine divine at the end of a ceremony.

★   Banishing the Guardians of the Four Cardinal Points

The guardians who were invoked at the start of the ceremony are thanked and asked to return to their own realms.

★   Opening the Circle

The circle is banished and the ritual space returned to its former situation. If outdoors, the tools are packed away and all evidence of a ceremony removed.

HISTORICAL ORIGINS

The practices and beliefs of the Wiccan tradition as it is known today, originate from a number of sources and were inspired by many individuals during the late nineteenth and early twentieth centuries. Debate on whether or not it was a constructed tradition or whether it is the remains of an older magickal tradition, will probably be with us for an eternity. What is clear is that certain authors and magickal traditions did have a greater influence on the material taught in the tradition today than others. Here we will consider the most important influences on the tradition:

Classical Paganism

Witchcraft is not a recent phenomenon; there are references to witches found in literature from around the world, dating back many hundreds and sometimes thousands of years. Examples of these can be found in ancient Greek and Roman writings, as well as in the Christian Bible. These witches were usually portrayed as solitary figures living on the fringes of society, feared but useful at times. Thus in the Old Testament we see Saul going to the Witch of Endor to conjure up the shade of the prophet Samuel.

Witchcraft of the Middle Ages

Many pagans refer to the Middle Ages as the *'Burning Times'* due to the witch trials that went on then. The witch trials came about following the persecution of large numbers of peasants resulting from accusations of witchcraft practices. Although the content of confessions extracted from alleged *'witches'* under torture must be considered as highly questionable, they do hint at practices existing at the time. However details written by the witches themselves have never been found so this remains an area of speculation.

In England however there was a tradition of *'cunning-men'* and *'cunning-women'* that practiced a mixture of folk magick combined with fragments of ceremonial magick from Grimoires and Qabalah. These cunning-folk practiced the arts commonly associated with witches, such as healing, love spells, finding lost objects, curses and their removal, etc. It is here that we may find most of the origins for the practices found in the Wiccan tradition and as such it is possible that Wicca might be a continuation of the old Grimoire Traditions, with the addition of pagan and hermetic beliefs at a later date. This is investigated in great detail in the book *Wicca Magickal Beginnings*.

The Grimoire Tradition

The Grimoire tradition refers to a collection of magickal texts from the thirteenth – eighteenth century which have been hugely influential in the development of many magickal traditions, including Wicca. The Grimoires were usually books of practice, containing instructions such as how to create magick circles, make the tools and incenses, perform the preparatory practices and how to conjure angels and demons to perform tasks for the magician.

Although they may appear very Christian in their theology with the one God and angels and demons below him, in fact there is a strong influence from Classical Paganism into the Grimoires. This can be seen both in the planetary nature of most of the Grimoires, which concentrate on spiritual creatures associated with the seven classical planets and their corresponding powers, and also the inclusion of faeries, elementals and other beings in some of them. The Grimoires drew from earlier traditions such as those of ancient Greece and the Qabalah, and so you can see that they acted as a bridge between the magick of the ancient world and that of modern times.

Charles Godfrey Leland

Leland was the American anthropologist who published *Aradia: Gospel of the Witches* in 1899. This book details the practices of Italian Witches from the Tuscany region who Leland believed to be part of a tradition with an unbroken lineage of practice going back a thousand years. Certainly Italian literature records belief in a cult of Diana going back many centuries, so this idea is not as farfetched as it might seem.

This book starts with the story of how the Goddess Diana joins in love with the God of Light and Splendour and produces a daughter, Aradia who is sent to Earth to teach mankind the arts of Witchcraft. Leland also produced a number of other interesting works, including *"Gipsy Sorcery"*, but it is *"Aradia"* that would be the most influential on the modern Wiccan Tradition, providing the prototype for part of the important Charge of the Goddess text in the first chapter entitled *"How Diana gave birth to Aradia"*.

The Golden Dawn

The Hermetic Order of the Golden Dawn was founded in 1887. It was a magickal order founded by three freemasons based on an amalgam of Renaissance magick, Hermeticism, Rosicrucianism, Alchemy, Qabalah and the Egyptian Gods. The Golden Dawn had a number of famous and influential members, including S.L. MacGregor Mathers, Aleister Crowley, W.B. Yeats, A.E. Waite, Florence Farr, Arthur Machen and many others. Its influence on subsequent magickal traditions has been significant for a number of reasons, including the legacy of material, both in scope and quantity, and the equality of male and female members. They produced rituals such as the Lesser Banishing Ritual of the Pentagram, which has provided inspiration for Wiccan Ritual and is sometimes still used in some traditions today. Additionally correspondences, tools and ritual techniques from the Golden Dawn have also made their way into Wicca.

Aleister Crowley

It is often said that you either love or hate Aleister Crowley and his work, which is a very harsh but true statement. Whatever you think of him, this Victorian magickian was and continues to be one of the most influential figures in the history of magick in the twentieth and twenty-first centuries. He was a member of the Hermetic Order of the Golden Dawn, and subsequently became the head of the Ordo

Templi Orientis (OTO). He used the OTO as a vessel to promote the Law of Thelema, which is encapsulated in the phrase: *"Do what thou wilt shall be the whole of the Law: Love is the Law, Love under Will"*. This phrase may have provided inspiration for the Wiccan Rede *"An it harm none – do as ye will"*.

Gerald Gardner met Crowley on a number of occasions before Crowley's death in 1947, and the inclusion of large chunks of text written and published by Aleister Crowley in some of the earlier Gardnerian rituals has given rise to a rumour that it may have been Crowley who wrote all the rituals of Wicca. This is another of those claims that cannot be substantiated. Although credit must be given where credit is due and a study of some of the key Wiccan texts does produce evidence that Crowley's work must at the very least have been a great inspiration for Gardner (and Doreen Valiente). Quotations from *"The Book of the Law"* (Liber Al vel Legis) and *"The Gnostic Mass"* can be found littered throughout some of the rituals of the tradition, including the *Charge of the Goddess* and *The Great Rite*.

Margaret Murray

In her books *The Witch Cult in Western Europe* (1921) and *God of the Witches* (1933) the British anthropologist Margaret Murray presented a view that medieval witchcraft was a survival of older Pagan religions. Though the material presented in these books is widely disputed today by scholars, regardless we cannot ignore the influence of her work on the Wiccan movement. Murray wrote the introduction for Gardner's book *Witchcraft Today,* and although her material is not actually significantly present in Wicca, it is obvious that the flavour of her writings influenced him and his contemporaries and continues to inspire some modern writers.

Dion Fortune

The British occultist Dion Fortune was born Violet Mary Firth in North Wales around 1890/1891. She joined one of the offshoots of the *Hermetic Order of the Golden Dawn* and later founded *The Society of the Inner Light*. Her contribution to the development of magick during the twentieth century is undisputed through books such as *Psychic Self-Defence* and her classic work *The Mystical Qabalah*. It was however through her fictional works, in particular *The Sea Priestess* and *Moon Magic* that she would provide a lasting influence on the Wiccan movement. These books present the story of a Priestess of Isis (The Egyptian Mother Goddess) who is trying to perpetuate and revive the worship of the Old Gods, especially that of Isis. Elements of the philosophies presented in this book, as well as rituals drawing from those presented in these books, have found their way into Wicca.

Robert Graves

During 1949 Robert Graves published his poetic work *The White Goddess*. This book presented many ideas that were to be incorporated into Wicca. Notably he made popular the concept of the triple Goddess as maiden, mother and crone which is used in many modern Pagan traditions. His work is however considered to be poetic, rather than historical.

Gerald Gardner

In 1949 Gerald Gardner published the fictional novel *High Magic's Aid* through which he introduced some of the practices of what would become known as the Wiccan Tradition for the first time. With a lifelong fascination for folklore, Gardner studied the myths and legends of different parts of the world throughout his life. He lived in diverse parts of the world and it was upon retirement in England that he claimed that he was initiated into a coven in the New Forest area of England in 1939, which he believed to be a survival of an older Pagan Witch Cult.

After the Fraudulent Mediums Act of 1951 was passed, it enabled Gardner and others who practiced magick to be open about their practices and beliefs for the first time without fear of prosecution. This act repealed the Witchcraft Act of 1735. As a result of this, Gardner was able to publish subsequent works without resorting to the guise of fiction, and to openly proclaim that he was a witch. Through the publication of his books such as *The Meaning of Witchcraft* and *Witchcraft Today* Gardner proceeded to make public some of the practices and beliefs of the coven he belonged to, though he was oathbound to only reveal certain parts of it. Gerald Gardner is often referred to as the *"Father of Modern Witchcraft"* and rightly so, as it was through his work and his initiates that the modern movement was created. He produced a Book of Shadows, which he claimed contained the rituals of Witchcraft, though only in fragmentary form, so he also included workings adapted from other magickal books available at the time, including notably the writings of Aleister Crowley. This he blended with ideas from folklore and mythology to create the basis for many of the ritual practices and ideas which we still have today. He worked with a number of High Priestesses, many of whom would continue his work of making available material and teachings of the Craft to new generations interested in the tradition.

Doreen Valiente

In 1953 Doreen Valiente was initiated by Gardner and was to become one of his best known High Priestesses through the work she did by rewriting his Book of Shadows, in particular the popular *Charge of the Goddess*. She left the Gardnerian movement as she was increasingly unhappy with what she viewed as Gardner's attempts to publicise Wicca and her own personal need for a more traditional approach to Witchcraft. Today she is sometimes called the *"Mother of Modern Witchcraft"* for the work she did both with Gardner and subsequently with Robert Cochrane. She wrote a number of books which continue to be influential today, including *An ABC of Witchcraft* (1973) and *Witchcraft for Tomorrow* (1978).

Alex & Maxine Sanders

In the 60's Alex Sanders teamed up with Maxine Morris (whom he later married) and moved to London. Alex and Maxine started covens in London, publicly initiating people and courting publicity through the media. They initiated large numbers of people, and Wicca expanded largely through their efforts, resulting in the formation of a large number of covens. Alexandrians today tended to be more eclectic and incorporate more ceremonial magick into their practices.

Janet and Stewart Farrar

The authors of *The Witches Bible* were originally initiated by Alex and Maxine Sanders. Their work was inspired not only by what they learned from the Sanders' but also through their correspondence with Doreen Valiente. Their work and research was to inspire many to create their own covens, initiating themselves and members of their groups using the rituals published in the aforementioned book (or variations thereof).

Exercise 1.3 – the Wiccan Timeline

Create a magickal timeline in your magickal diary, noting the important dates, events and people that have contributed to the development of the Wiccan tradition in the last 100-150 years. Be sure to give yourself plenty of space, you may even prepare it in rough first and then copy it in when you are happy with it.

Wicca: Recent Decades

Since the 1970's a number of new traditions of Wicca have emerged, mostly founded on the work done by those who inspired Gerald Gardner or those who were inspired by them. Some groups have invented new traditions, using the term 'Wicca' and in some instances making claims that their tradition predates that of Gerald Gardner's – in most instances these claims seems to be fabrications of the founders, though the jury is still out on some.

Others have created traditions which draw heavily on one aspect of the tradition – such as the feminine Divine, whilst not necessarily dismissing the other components; others have dismissed large sections of the original teachings in favour of new mythologies, new and sometimes progressive ideas. Ultimately many of these traditions still draw heavily on the material first made available through the writings and teachings of Gerald Gardner and/or Alex and Maxine Sanders; following a ritual liturgy akin that roughly outlined earlier in this chapter, celebrating the seasonal festivals and working their magick in the light of the Moon.

There has been and will continue to be much controversy about the exact origins of the Wiccan Tradition. Did Gerald Gardner *"make it all up"* or was there really a *New Forest Coven*? Were the rituals Gerald Gardner used actually written by Aleister Crowley as some researchers suggest? Is Wicca the true continuation of an older European Witch Cult? The debate is likely to rage on for many years to come, unless conclusive new evidence emerges.

More importantly though, it is important for those who choose Wicca as their spiritual and magickal path today to remember that regardless of its origins, Wicca is a beautiful and valid spiritual path and an effective magickal tradition. It is firmly rooted in the Western Mystery Tradition and through it into the practices and beliefs of many ancient cultures. It has a great deal to offer those who explore its practices and gain knowledge through experience! Wicca is more than the sum of its parts, it is a Craft, and just like other forms of art, it can never be learned from a book alone – it can only be learned from personal experience which comes through practice and hard work, in addition to study.

Exercise 1.4 - Your Personal Timeline

Which significant events in your life brought you to the Wiccan path? List these events and where possible the time of year they happened, creating a timeline. This might include a wide range of occurrences, such as dreams, people you met, events you attended, ceremonies you performed, etc.

Does a particular season or Sabbat stand out as significantly connected with these events? If so, make a note so you can look at the associated themes and explore their relevance to your path.

Exercise 1.5 – Chakra Work

In Appendix 5 you will find information about working with your chakras, which are energy centres in your subtle body. Try the exercises in this appendix, working through them and trying each one for at least several consecutive days. Note exercises 2 and 3 to open and close the chakras should be practiced together.

Key Points

★ The terms Wicca, Witchcraft and Paganism all have different uses and meanings.

★ Wicca is an experiential Mystery Tradition which began as an initiatory tradition, but is now also practiced by a very large number of solitary practitioners.

★ Wiccans honour the masculine and feminine divine, and celebrate the changing seasons through the Sabbat festivals.

★ There is a standard ritual format which is practiced by the majority of groups and individuals calling themselves Wiccan

---

Further Suggested Reading:

★ *Firechild* by Maxine Sanders
★ *Gerald Gardner and the Cauldron of Inspiration* by Philip Heselton
★ *King of the Witches* (Biography of Alex Sanders) by June Johns
★ *Triumph of the Moon* by Prof. Ronald Hutton
★ *Wicca Magickal Beginnings* by Sorita d'Este and David Rankine
★ *Wiccan Roots* by Philip Heselton

LESSON 2

MAGICK: TOWARDS AN UNDERSTANDING

To understand Magick you must first forget all the fallacies and stereotypical preconceptions taught to you out of fear and ignorance and approach this subject with an open mind. You will probably find it is not what you have been taught to think! Magick has been defined as *"The art and science of causing change to occur in conformity with will"*, and also that *"magick is conscious evolution through directing energy."*

Similarly, magick is about focusing more subtle, non-physical energies that cannot usually be seen, and directing them to create change. To go about this requires experience, and training to improve the power of the mind, and specifically, the will. Acts such as meditation, breath control, voice work, visualization, ritual, and others, are all designed to improve the body and mind, to produce clarity and balance, and to enable perception and wielding of more subtle energies. In the same way, an individual is as strong as their will, and the more balanced and integrated a person is, the stronger their will.

Practising magick tends to act as a deconditioning mechanism and can be a subtle process, the longer the period of time you spend practicing it, the more positive change you experience through the removal of the unnecessary inhibitions, stigmas, guilt and sin complexes that society builds in. This has the effect of releasing the energy that has been spent perpetuating negative conditioning back into the psyche, where it can strengthen you, the individual.

Magickal training and experience bring forth the energies of the unconscious, and so it is no surprise to see that symbols become more important as you develop, providing not only the language of dreams and the unconscious, but also helping create a more flexible perception map of the universe. To grow spiritually, it is vital that you remain flexible and do not become dogmatic, rather that you are open to experience and willing to question your ideas and beliefs as a result of those experiences. Magick can be a painful process. It is not easy to maintain the discipline and honest self-critical approach all the time. It can also be hard work dealing with the energy released without being knocked off balance sometimes.

"Magic" or "Magick"

Some people ask why magick is spelt with a 'k' on the end. The primary reason for doing this is to help distinguish it from the magic practised by illusionists and stage magicians. As Magick is not about illusion, but instead about creating real change, the use of the spelling ending in k distinguishes it and also provides an energetic separation from that practiced by stage magicians. Historically it was used as *"magic"* or *"magick"* interchangeably, prior to the standardisation of the English language. As such neither is a modern invention, but the reintroduction of the 'k' simply helps to clarify the term for use by Wiccans and other practitioners of spiritual and results related magick. The spelling of *"magick"* is sometimes attributed to Aleister Crowley, but although credit can be given to him for making this popular through his use of it in his writings, he certainly did not invent it as it appears in this way in many old manuscripts and books prior to Crowley's writing and contemporary with it, including scientific books. Thus we see the spelling in works such as *"History of Magick"* (1657), *"A Compleat History of Magick, Sorcery and Witchcraft"* (1715-16) and *"To describe the construction of the magick lantern"* (1811).

As an aside though, it is interestingly, 'k' is also the eleventh letter of the alphabet, and eleven is considered to be the number of magick. The reason for this is that it is one beyond the perfect ten, considered perfect as our numerical system works in base ten, and as such can be seen to represent the unseen or hidden energies and beings in the world around us.

Towards the Wiccan Circle

Wiccan Results Magick

Wiccans use magick to create positive transformation and change. This transformation and change is brought on both in our own lives, as well as in the world around us.

Results magick worked by Wiccans may include spells and ceremonies to achieve:

* ★ Healing Work
* ★ Personal transformation
* ★ Protection
* ★ Blessings
* ★ Attraction (Results) Magick
* ★ Purification and consecrations
* ★ Trance, Astral Projection and shapeshifting

There are many different magickal traditions, each of which has their own way of creating magick and raising power for the purpose. Wiccans usually perform their magick in a circle and may raise energy to empower their magick through different methods, which are sometimes combined for best effect. These methods may include:

* ★ Concentration & Visualisation
* ★ Different trance states
* ★ Herbs and Incense
* ★ Dance and movement
* ★ Voice work (e.g. Chanting)
* ★ Breath work

Exercise 2.1 – Defining Magick

How would you define magick? Consider what magick means to you, and how you think it works, and try to find a definition that you are happy with. When you have done so, write the definition in your magickal diary.

---

page 33

WICCAN MAGICK TOOLS

Today a wide variety of magickal tools can be bought in shops from anywhere in the world but this was not always the case. They are available in all shapes and sizes and can even be bought by mail-order or on the internet, but it has to be said that there is definitely something in the old belief held by some practitioners of the magickal arts that you should make your own tools, or have them made by a crafts person who understands the workings of magick. Although they may be more expensive, these tools are empowered whilst they are made and will make for far more effective magickal tools when used than the equivalent which was mass produced in a factory for the New Age market. There are a number of tools which are used on a regular basis in Wiccan ceremonies. These include:

★ Athame – a ritual dagger, traditionally with a black hilt and double edged blade. Represents the will of the individual practitioner and is sometimes known as *'the real witch's weapon'*. Used to cast the magick circle, for consecrations, to direct energy and for invocations. Symbolic of the Masculine divine and the element of Fire.

★ Wand – made from wood or sometimes, from stone (crystal) or metal. When wooden it is traditionally made from a fruit or nut bearing tree, and should be made by the person who will be using it. Symbolic of the masculine divine, and used for many of the same purposes of the athame, to direct energy, invocations, consecrations etc.

★ Pentacle – made from metal, wax or wood. It is used as the basis for consecrations, i.e. they are performed by placing the item on the pentacle. Traditionally inscribed with a pentagram. Symbolic of the element of Earth.

★ Censer (Incense) – any container, in which incense is burned, should be fireproof! Used for a range of purposes, including focus, devotion, healing and skrying. Symbolic of the element of Air

★ Chalice – a cup, this can be any cup set aside for use in ritual, usually silver, stone or wood. It is used to hold the sacramental wine, or may be used to hold water or other liquids. Symbolic of the Feminine divine and the element of Water.

The following tools may also be used by some Wiccans:

★ Cords – used for knot magick, binding and tied around the waist during ceremonies.

★ White Handled Knife – used for carving sigils on candles and other tools. As the name suggests a knife with a white handle. If you plan on using this tool make sure that it is practical for you to use. Symbolic of the element of Air.

★ Sickle – not a *"traditional"* Wiccan tool, but used sometimes to represent the harvest or the Moon. Sometimes this is used to cut herbs with, although it is certainly not the most practical tool for the job!

★ Cauldron – not a tool as such, but sometimes used as symbolic of the *"Cauldron of Ceridwen"* in which this Goddess brewed a magick potion in the tale of Taliesin, also symbolic of *"the womb of the Goddess"*. It can be used to burn things in, and sometimes to light a fire indoors (though care should be taken when doing this!)

★ Ceremonial Sword – not normally necessary for solitary work and when used in a coven it is usual for there to be just one sword, representing the *"Will"* of the group. The sword is used to direct energy and for invocations – in a similar way to the athame or wand. Symbolic of the element of Spirit and also represents authority.

Ritual tools are all purified (i.e. cleansed) and then consecrated before use in ceremonies. The process of consecration charges or empowers an object with energy to make it effective for use in magickal work, and creates a magickal link between you and your tool.

Exercise 2.2 – the Tools

List the all the tools which might be used in Wicca, together with their symbolism, uses and other notes in your magickal diary.

SKYCLAD OR ROBED

Many Wiccans perform their ceremonies skyclad, that is to say naked, though many will wear robes (and sometimes cloaks) when it is cold or impractical to work skyclad. It is necessary to clarify here that traditional Wiccan covens will only work skyclad when they are working with other initiates, some may only work skyclad when the weather permits or when they are working indoors. This is usually a matter of choice decided by the coven and its leaders. Some prefer to always work skyclad, others prefer to work robed.

Those groups which opt for working in robes will generally decide to wear the same colour (and sometimes the same design) robes, often opting for the traditional black, long-sleeved, ankle-length robes (sometimes with hoods). The reason for choosing a dark colour is one of practicality, as it allows for anonymity and invisibility when working outdoors and of course doesn't show dirt as much as a white robe (for example) would. Many also choose green for the same reason.

Here are some of the reasons given in support of skyclad working:

★ That robes or clothes inhibit the power latent in the body
★ That being skyclad creates equality amongst members of a coven
★ That it helps us to leave the mundane behind.
★ That working skyclad helps individuals to shed their inhibitions.

One of the key reasons for working skyclad or for wearing uniformed robes is to encourage the members of a coven to cast aside their social and economic selves, prior to entering into the circle. By being skyclad or robed, everyone is equal and by changing out of their mundane clothing each member casts of those differences before stepping into the circle. It also forms part of the magickal transformation and development of the magickal self, in which the practitioners of magick becomes the perfected self, focused entirely on the work at hand, rather than being reminded of everyday concerns.

Those working their magick alone can decide for themselves how they wish to present themselves in their circle, as there is obviously no peer group to be equal or superior to. The same importance should however be placed on casting aside the mundane, before stepping into the circle, in order to gain the maximum benefits and to help the practitioners assume their magickal personality more readily.

If the only reason to remove clothing for ritual is to ensure that the energy can escape then there are a number of problems with this theory. Firstly, if the energy in the first place is so weak as to be prevented from permeating a thin layer of clothing, then is there much point in performing the ceremonies at all? It would also bring into question how successful magick is being done by many other magickal traditions, who usually all wear robes!

Being skyclad may promote the idea of equality amongst members, but the same effect would be created through the use of uniform robes (i.e. everyone wearing a similar pattern robe, in the same colour). In the same way as being skyclad helps us to leave the mundane behind and prepare ourselves better for doing magickal work, so robes can have exactly the same effect.

Shedding inhibitions is probably higher on the list of possible answers. In order for the individual to grow magickally they need to let go of their 'old' selves in order to foster a better relationship with the new, reborn magickal self. Many people in the Western World have body image problems and often this features high on the list of fears that would-be initiates have. By overcoming this fear we take a step towards shedding our old selves and replacing it with the new one who can and will grow. However of course, just taking your clothes of is not going to be quite enough.

Instead of working skyclad someone may decide to have another *"special"* outfit, or item (such as jewellery, a scarf etc) which you only wear when you doing ritual. You may of course have other bits of magickal jewellery which you can wear for either ritual or every day.

Being skyclad does of course also have the added benefits of not having to worry about setting your robes on fire (which can, believe it or not, be a real problem!).

Exercise 2.3 – Skyclad or Robed

What do you see as the benefits and pitfalls of working skyclad?
List these and give some thought to your own personal feelings
towards working skyclad for rituals. Examine your reasons for feeling
positive or negative towards the practice carefully.

ETHICS OF WICCAN MAGICK

"An it Harm None – Do as you Will"

The Wiccan Rede is the moral code or *"golden rule"* of the Wiccan Tradition. There are many different versions in circulation, including some long and poetic versions, but the eight words as given above can be considered to be the Wiccan Rede, with the occasional variation of the *"you"* as a *"ye"*. Regardless of the version of the eight words you take for consideration, or if you like to develop your own in time, having a golden rule to measure your actions by can be a valuable guide when you decide to wield the power of magickal work. This becomes even more important if you work alone as you will not have a peer group to help keep you balanced and grounded.

The word Rede is an archaic word meaning *"to give advice or council"* and as such we can translate the phrase to mean *"advice for Wiccans"*. It is not a rule, but rather some advice from those who have walked this path before us. Each individual should interpret the Wiccan Rede for themselves, it is not a charter to do whatever you feel like doing; instead it stresses personal responsibility. It is your responsibility to *"harm none"* when you *"do as you will"*. It is your responsibility to figure out what it means to do your will. And it is you who have to take responsibility for the fruits of all your own actions – good, bad or indifferent; magickal or mundane.

"The Wiccan Rede provides you with a personal guideline which you can use whenever you need to make an important decision. Not just decisions in regard to magickal workings, but also in your every day life. The Wiccan Rede places the emphasis on personal responsibility for all your actions. It says 'hold on a minute, do you need to do that? How will your actions affect you? Are you sure you want to go ahead?"[3]

Taking personal responsibility means that you cannot blame anyone or anything else for your actions. You are responsible for the

---

[3] Circle of Fire, Sorita d'Este and David Rankine

things you cause to others, and your environment as well as to yourself. Although of course we are influenced by what happened to us as children or how we were treated by parents and teachers, personal responsibility means taking active decisions to make positive changes to our lives.

You have to make decisions about your own life, regardless of peer pressure, decisions that reflect what you need in your life. It might seem harsh when you first think about it, but applying this philosophy to your life will bring about positive changes for you and is less harmful in the long term. By applying the Rede to your actions you are forced to examine your own ethics. This helps you work out what your views and beliefs on different issues are, and thus develop a sharper picture of your worldview. The importance of the Wiccan Rede today is clearly illustrated through its use in a variety of modern Pagan traditions and the wide variety of variants being used. Its popularity seems to stem from the need for a moral guideline which often manifests in a fear of the uncertainty that practising magick may bring to one's life.

In addition to the Wiccan Rede, some Wiccans look to the *Charge of the Goddess* for moral guidance. For this the following lines are particularly apt:

> *"Keep pure your highest ideal;*
> *strive ever towards it, let naught stop you or turn you aside…"*
> *"For my law, is love unto all beings…"*

These lines focus on the need to find and strive ever towards your own personal highest ideals; this means that you of course first need to establish what those ideals are – which is a process that might take a long time. It emphasises that we should be strong in our convictions that what we are doing is right, so much so that we should not allow ourselves to be dissuaded by obstacles in our path. It also highlights the nature of the law as love.

> *"Let there beauty and strength, power and compassion, honour and humility,*
> *mirth and reverence within you…"*

These are very high ideals to strive for and to integrate all of them into our lives might take many years of personal work and soul searching. It is a good measure against which to test our actions; is what we are about to do (magickal or mundane) something we can claim to be done with beauty and strength? Are we doing so with power and compassion, honour and humility? Does it show both mirth and reverence for those who will be affected and towards the Gods?

Exercise 2.4 – the Wiccan Rede

How do you feel the Wiccan Rede relates to your life? Do you feel it is relevant to your life and follow it?

Or is there a different 'Golden Rule' that you live by?

When considering these questions consider the implications of the Rede on what you eat and drink, what you buy, how you dispose of household waste, how you treat your family, friends and work colleagues?

If you wish you can extend this to how you view the legal system and how people are treated for committing different crimes.

VISUALISATION

In order to manifest our magick, we need to be able to *'see'* our desired outcome. To do this one of the first skills that we need to learn is visualisation. We also need to be able to still our minds to enable us to focus purely on the work we are doing during a ceremony, in order to have complete focus. Visualisation is a skill that, like any other, is something that some find very easy and others may struggle with at first – it is however something that can be learned and which can be improved through practice. Visualisation is a skill that is used in all areas of life. Creative people often visualise the desired outcome to a project in order for them to create it and successful business people may do the same in order for them to succeed and create effective business plans. In the same way a gardener may visualise the layout of their garden by, for example, *"seeing"* the small sapling they are about to plant as a fully grown tree, allowing them to allow sufficient space for the tree to grow and develop in, without disturbing other plants or structures. Visualisation is one of the keys to successful magickal work and as such is one that should be practiced on a regular basis. To test your own abilities, try the following exercise:

Take a few deep breaths. If you want, you can close your eyes. Relax and make sure that you are comfortable. Now think of one person in your life. This could be your relative, a friend, a lover or someone you work with. Try and see their face in your minds' eye, what colours is their hair and their eyes? Think of the shape of their face – is it round, oval or maybe it is heart shaped? Now try and see them standing somewhere that you know they are familiar with, maybe the last place you saw them. Try and visualise their clothes, posture and all other details you can remember. Think of how tall or short they are - what distinguishing features they have. Do they wear particular items of jewellery?

When you have done this you can relax again and make notes about the experience – did you struggle to see some of their features? Did you see them happy, sad, or angry? Did you find it difficult to keep the location they were standing in from changing? Maybe you found it easy and were able to clearly see a detailed image of them?

This will be different for everyone and it is important to be honest with yourself about the results you achieved to enable you to work on and develop this skill as much as possible.

If you struggled to visualise the person, choose someone that you have a photograph of. Study the photograph and then visualise them. If you still struggle, open your eyes to remind yourself of the details and take in details you may have missed or that did not come to you when you were visualising them. Leave it for an hour or two and try and visualise them again. Was this easier or harder? If you can master the art of being able to clearly see people, it will be easier for you to visualise other things. You can try this exercise with any image, many choose to use Tarot (or Oracle) cards, a favourite place or tree. You can use any object, including things you have in the room you are in at the moment - chairs, cups, musical instruments, book covers etc.

Preparation

Before visualising, or any form of meditation, you should make sure you are in the best state you can be. This means being comfortable in your position to minimise physical distractions. Sitting upright in a chair, or cross-legged on the floor are preferable, with your spine straight in either case. Lying down is not a good idea as you may fall asleep as you relax. Close your eyes and take a few deep breaths. You may then begin your exercise. When you are visualising an object, unless specifically indicated otherwise, see the background as a wall of black or white, whichever works better for you.

Exercise 2.5 – The Triangle

Visualise and hold in your mind's eye the image of a red equilateral triangle, point upwards on a black background. Try and keep this image focused and still for a minute. Once you manage to keep it still for one minute, continue practising until you can keep the image for five minutes. Whilst you hold the image in your mind's eye it should not change shape or colour, but be completely still. If you struggle with this at first, it might be useful to create a visual aid by drawing the triangle onto a piece of card which you can use to focus on.

Exercise 2.6 – The Tree

In Appendix 4 you will find The Tree exercise. Perform this for at least three consecutive days to help you develop your visualisation skills (more days is good if you wish to). Record in your magickal diary what feelings you experience in your body and mind as you perform this exercise, which is a very useful balancing and energising practice.

Exercise 2.7 – The Fruit

Visualise and hold in your mind's eye the image of your favourite fruit. As well as seeing its shape and colour, take note also of its texture and add the smell of the fruit into your visualisation. Start at a minute and again build up until you can hold the image for 5 minutes, seeing it from different angles without it changing shape or colour.

Exercise 2.8 – The Pentagram

See a golden pentagram, point upwards, on a black background. Keep the image clear and focused for at least a minute, and then see golden flames coming off the pentagram, which maintains its original shape. See the flames dancing for a few minutes, and then see them die down so you are left with just the original pentagram.

SYMBOLS OF WICCA

A symbol is an image, picture, sign, term, word or action which we may be familiar with in daily life, but which has more meanings than are immediately obvious. Symbols imply something vague, unknown or hidden from us. They speak to, and emerge from, our unconscious minds, and are never precisely defined or fully explained by rational thought. By working with symbols our minds are led to ideas beyond the grasp of reason, and this can lead to transcendent experience. From the beginning it is necessary to keep in mind that regardless of how strong a particular association with a particular symbol is in one culture and at one time, one concept will often be represented with many different symbols. To make things even more confusing, the same symbol may mean many different things in different cultures at different times.

For this reason, if you decide to work with symbols in your magickal work, it is necessary to choose a set to work with from the outset, embedding their meanings firmly in your mind so that you may use them effectively in your magick. It is of course possible to add to those symbols over a period of time, learning alternatives and using both together, but if you wish to use symbolism then it would be unwise to confuse your mind with too many alternatives at the start, as you will not be able to connect with them on the same deep level as when you focus on one set first.

Although some background and explanation is given for these symbols, bear in mind that a symbol always means more than can be expressed in words. It is up to you to explore these symbols for yourself, and see how they affect you, what experiences they bring you, and how they speak to your unconscious.

Goddess Symbols

 The crescent moon is the classic Wiccan Goddess symbol, representing the lunar tides and flows. Although the Goddess is not just the Moon, this symbol from alchemy has become the standard symbol for Her.

Likewise a circle with crescents on either side is also used to depict the Goddess, in Her triple aspect of Maiden, Mother and Crone, represented by the waxing, full and waning moon shown in the image. Other images associated with the Goddess in Wicca include: the Circle, the Chalice, the Cauldron and Lilies.

God Symbols

The symbol for Taurus, i.e. a circle with a crescent on its side on top like horns, is the most common symbol used to represent the Horned God. For though Taurus is the bull (with horns), it is ruled by the planet Venus, symbolising the love of the Goddess.

The Sun symbol of a circle with a dot in the middle is also sometimes used to represent the fiery masculine energy of the God, balancing the watery lunar energy of the Goddess. Again this depiction probably comes from medieval alchemy. Other symbols used to represent the God in Wicca may include: Pine cones, the Wand, the Athame and other phallic representations.

The Pentagram

Many volumes could be written on the symbolism of the pentagram! The Pentagram is an ancient symbol used throughout history to represent many different things and has been persistent in its appearance and use within magickal and spiritual traditions for many thousands of years. It has been found in the literature, relics and art from numerous cultures from countless periods in history – from the ancient Babylonians, Chinese, Egyptians, Greeks, Indians, Jewish to the Mayans, Christians and more recently modern Pagan traditions. In the Wiccan tradition it is taken to represents the four elements (Air, Fire, Water & Earth) in perfect balance thereby creating the fifth element, that of Spirit. It has become a symbol which is used to represent the Wiccan tradition, as well as a number of other modern Pagan traditions in more recent times.

As the Pentagram is created from one single line it has also become a symbol of both perfection and infinity. As such it brings these energies with it when used in the magick circle. In Wiccan ritual it is used for consecrations, blessings and invocations. It is usually inscribed on the Pentacle as well as optionally on some of the other tools during their consecrations. Elemental Pentagrams are often used in the invocation and banishing of the Watchtowers – or the Guardians of the Four Elemental realms within ceremonies. These are invoked at the appropriate cardinal points of the magick circle which are:

* Air – East
* Fire – South
* Water – West
* Earth – North

It represents the expression of the four cardinal points, plus the fifth point, the centre; manifesting the five elements, Earth, Air, Fire, Water, and Spirit.

Upright it shows Spirit above matter, and is a symbol of the Goddess and Woman. Inverted it shows Matter above Spirit, or Spirit made manifest in Matter, and is a symbol of the Horned God. Inverted it is also used a symbol for the Second Degree Priestesses and Priests. It also symbolizes the five senses, five limbs and five fingers or toes.

The Hexagram

The hexagram, or six-pointed star, represents the Universe. It also encapsulates the axiom *"As Above, So Below"* which is represented by its two interlocking triangles, one pointing up and one pointing down. The downward pointing triangle represents the Goddess and the element of Water, the upward pointing triangle represents the God and the element of Fire. The upward pointing triangle, combined with the horizontal baseline of the other triangle, represents the element of Air. The downward pointing triangle with the horizontal line of the upwards pointing triangle represents the element of Earth. Thus the hexagram combines the symbols of all four of the elements, which comprise the totality of the material universe. The Hexagram is also sometimes called *"The Star of David"* and is a sacred symbol of Judaism.

SYMBOLISM

Whilst symbols are pictorial representations of ideas, many things can have symbolism, such as colours, numbers or scents. When things have a symbolism relating to a particular concept, such as an element or planet, it is known as a correspondence. The use of correspondences is particularly found in one of the classic magickal principles, that of sympathetic magick. Sympathetic magick works on the principle that an item which has a symbolic correspondence to something or has had actual contact with that thing, can be used to exert an influence on that thing from a distance. In the Middle Ages a form of this was postulated by the doctor-magician Paracelsus, known as the *"Doctrine of Signatures"*, and this forms the basis of many of the correspondences used for healing herbs, through their colours and shapes.

Symbolism plays a major role in Wiccan ceremonies. The colours of items, the number of times you do things, the scents you use, everything you do and use has relevance on a symbolic level through their correspondences. Let us say you were performing a Venusian ritual, to use as much appropriate symbolism as possible you might wear a green robe and have a green altar cloth and candles, anoint yourself with rose oil, burn benzoin gum as an incense, have a rose on your altar, wear a green cord to symbolise the Venusian girdle, recite chants a multiple of seven times (the number of Venus). Every extra layer of symbolism adds to the focusing of the mind on the energy you are working with. To understand this, it is necessary to continue thinking of the magick you are doing as a Craft, something which you need to specialise in, practice and hone your skills in, in order to be good at it. Wiccan magick is indeed a Craft, and even after years of practice you should still continue to discover new levels of meaning to the symbolism found in its ceremonies. (And if you are not, it could be argued that you are doing something wrong!)

Exercise 2.9 - Symbols

Draw the Pentagram, Hexagram, Goddess and God symbols into your magickal diary, and add your thoughts about each of them. Periodically revisit these pages, say every two months, and see how your perceptions have changed. You may wish to leave some space to add future insights about the symbols as you gain them.

Key Points

★ Wicca is a magickal tradition, and so the practice of magick is an integral part of being Wiccan.

★ The basic Wiccan tools represent the elements and are used regularly in ceremonies. There are other tools whose use is optional.

★ All tools should be purified prior to use to prepare them, and then consecrated to empower them and create a magickal link between you and the tool.

★ Wiccan rituals are usually performed robed or skyclad, according to preference.

★ The Wiccan Rede is an ethical guide that many Wiccans try to adhere to.

★ Visualisation is a vital skill for magickal work, and should be practiced so that you gain a proficiency in it to make your practices more successful.

★ Certain symbols are considered particularly significant in the Wiccan tradition.

Further Option Reading

★ *Circle of Fire* by Sorita d'Este and David Rankine
★ *Magic: an Occult Primer* by David Conway
★ *The Complete Magicians' Tables* by Stephen Skinner

LESSON 3

THE GODS & GODDESSES

Wiccans perceive the Divine as being expressed through a dualistic nature, as the divine feminine and divine masculine (goddess and god). The way in which the divine is perceived is based on personal experiences and perceptions and within the tradition as a whole, there are no fixed ways in which practitioners are expected to perceive the divine. The Goddess is usually seen as the giver of life, from whom all life was created and the God is seen as her lover and her consort. The focus of Wiccan spirituality furthermore placed on the union between the Divine Feminine and Masculine, and unlike some other modern pagan traditions, we usually invoke both a Goddess and a God when we perform our rites. There are of course times when we might work just with a Goddess or just with a God (just to confuse things a little!) but throughout the yearly cycle we will work with both Goddesses and Gods as is appropriate.

The Divine Masculine and Divine Feminine are also sometimes referred to generically as *"the Lord and Lady"* when people wish to work with them in their all-encompassing aspects without naming a particular form. We may note that Lord and Lady are also translations of the names of the Norse brother and sister deities Frey and Freya. With Frey being a fertility and agricultural god, and Freya being a love, fertility and battle goddess, the names of this pairing are interestingly appropriate. This is also a good illustration of where the *'name'* of a deity is in fact a *'title'* rather than a name, a theme which recurs throughout many of the world pantheons.

In addition to Frey and Freya's names, other good illustrations of this idea can be found in the names of the Celtic Irish Goddess the Morrígan, whose name means *'Great Queen'*. Likewise Cernunnos, the Horned God most often invoked in modern Wicca, can be translated as

'Horned One' a reference to the powerful bull horns (later stag) he is depicted with. There are many such examples and if you plan on working with a deity, a good starting point is always to find out what their name means and if they had any other known titles. These will provide you with valuable clues, which in turn will help you when you prepare to do our own personal ceremonies.

In Wicca the emphasis is placed on the balance between the Divine Feminine, often viewed as Lunar with Her Divine Masculine counterpart being a Horned God associated with Nature or sometimes a Sun God. The emphasis in Wicca is placed on duality and balance, on the joining of opposites, male and female, yin and yang, light and dark, through which balance and unity is achieved.

The Divine Feminine is often viewed as representing all of Nature - including the Earth, the Stars and of course the Moon. A name often used for the divine feminine in modern Wicca is that of Aradia, the daughter of the Roman Goddess Diana according to myths recorded in *The Aradia – Gospel of the Witches* by Charles G. Leland towards the end of the 1800's. Goddesses such as Diana, Hekate, Artemis, Ceridwen, Arianrhod, Bride (Brighid) and Isis are also often called upon in ceremonies. As traditionally many Wiccans view all Goddesses as being part of a Greater Universal Goddess and see the different names and faces of the Goddess as emanations of different archetypes – this means that in essence traditionally Wicca is a religion of duality, even though not all Wiccans necessarily see it that way.

THE GODDESS

Today many Wiccans, like other modern Pagan traditions, share a vision of the feminine Divine which was first expressed by Apuleius in his book *The Golden Ass* written in ancient Roman times. In this he expressed the belief that all the Goddesses are aspects of one Goddess. This view was made popular through the writings of Dion Fortune in her novels, *Sea Priestess* & *Moon Magic*, which were hugely influential on the modern Pagan movement:

"I am she who ere the earth was formed
Was Ea, Binah, Ge
I am that soundless, boundless, bitter sea,
Out of whose deeps life wells eternally.
Astarte, Aphrodite, Ashtoreth –
Giver of life and bringer of death;
Hera in Heaven, on earth, Persephone;
Levanah of the tides and Hecate –
All these am I, and they are seen in me…"

This view is the most prevalent in Wicca, and is certainly the one expressed in the Charge of the Goddess in the lines *"Listen to the words of the Great Mother; she who of old was also called among men Artemis, Astarte, Athene, Dione, Melusine, Aphrodite, Ceridwen, Dana, Arianrhod, Isis, Bride, and by many other names…"* The different Goddesses are seen as different aspects of the Divine Feminine, like different faces she wears to different people who approach her with different needs. The Divine Feminine is seen as being omnipresent and immortal. She is present in everything, and we are all part of Her body. She is the creatrix who gave birth to the God from Herself, and mated with Him to create the universe. In Wicca She is seen in a number of aspects – the Stellar Queen, Moon Goddess and Earth Goddess being the main ones.

"I am that secret queen, Persephone.
All tides are mine, and answer unto me.
Tides of the airs, tides of the inner earth,
The secret silent tides of death and birth –
Tides of men's souls, and dreams, and destiny-
Isis veiled and Rhea, Binah, Ge."

Moon Goddesses have long been seen as important, not only does the Moon rule the tides of the oceans and coincide with the cycles of women, it is also the great light in the night sky providing safety and light by which to travel, hunt, fish, perform spells, dream or many other activities.

Examples of Lunar Goddesses include:

★ Artemis / Diana - the Greek/Roman Virgin Goddess of the New Moon, Huntress and Divine Midwife.

★ Arianrhod - the Celtic Goddess of the Silver Circle, representing the face of the Moon, and also the Stars.

★ Hekate – the Greek triple Goddess of Magick and Witches, Queen of the Underworld, the only Titan Goddess to be honoured by Zeus, above all of the Olympian Gods.

★ Selene - the Moon Herself in the Greek pantheon, sister to Helios the Sun God.

The Divine Feminine in Wicca is also often viewed as the Mother Goddess. Again this is a matter that has caused a lot of confusion amongst those who want proof, history, etc. Some feminists who have been involved in the growth of and the popularity of the feminine divine in modern times have tried to promote the idea of one all mighty female Goddess who was worshipped and celebrated in ancient times. This Great Mother theory is unfortunately fraught with inaccuracies, but at the same time it is not entirely incorrect either. There were Mother Goddesses and Earth Goddesses in ancient times, quite often Earth Goddesses were also Mother Goddesses – but it remains that there were many, rather than just one and that in some instances they are significantly different from each other, even though some of them seem to have a lot of the same attributes, others are quite definitely distinct.

Examples of Mother Goddesses include:

★ Ceridwen - The Welsh Shape-shifting Goddess who is the mother of the beautiful Creirwy, Morvan and the ugly Avaggdu. She created a cauldron of inspiration which required tending for a year, but its virtue was accidentally absorbed by the boy Gwion Bach, whilst tending the cauldron for Ceridwen. After a shape shifting chase, he transformed into a kernel of grain and was eaten by Ceridwen as a hen. Months later Ceridwen gave birth to a baby boy who would in time become the bard Taliesin.

★ Danu - The Irish Mother Goddess after whom the pantheon of
the Tuatha de Danann are named. She is the wife of the
Ancestor God Bilé and the mother of the Daghda, Brian,
Iuchar and Iucharba.

★ Demeter – The Greek Goddess of the Grain and mother to
Persephone (Kore) who is abducted by Hades, the Lord of the
Underworld and becomes Queen of Hades (Underworld).
The relationship between Demeter and Persephone became
the focus of the famous Eleusian Mysteries, one of the best
known ancient Mystery Traditions, in which the seasons of
Nature are celebrated.

★ Don – The Welsh Mother Goddess who is the wife of the Sun
God Beli Mawr and mother to Arianrhod, Penarddun,
Gwydion, Gilvaethwy, Govannon, Amaethon (the Children
of Light) and Nudd.

★ Isis – The Egyptian Goddess of Magick. Isis is the wife/sister
of Osiris, a vegetation God, who becomes God of the
Underworld. Their child, Horus, was the God who took over
the kingship of his father, Osiris, resulting in the long series of
wars with his uncle, the God Set, about rightful succession as
King of the Gods.

Exercise 3.1 - Moon Goddess Meditation

Sit comfortably and relax, closing your eyes. In your mind's eye fix the image of yourself sitting as you are in the room. Hold this image, and then see a white mist filling the room, obscuring the walls, the floor, the ceiling, everything, until all around you is white mist. As the mist disperses you find yourself in a silver chariot pulled through the night sky by four silver horses.

Standing next to you in the chariot is a beautiful young woman with long silver hair and grey eyes in a flowing silver dress. A simple silver band holds her hair back off her face, and a necklace of moonstones hangs around her neck. As you glance at the necklace you realise the moonstones each show differing amounts of black and the luminescence of the stone, like the Moon herself in her phases. As silver light radiates from her face you realise that this is Selene, the moon goddess, travelling her course through the night sky. Her light dims a little, and as you look forward you see one of the front horses turns black.

You keep looking around, at the stars above, and the dimly lit landscape below, and as you do so her light dims again, and the other front horse turns black. You realise the phases of the moon are reflected through her light and the colour of her horses.

"Understanding the nature of cycles will help you move forward on your path," Selene tells you, *"the ebbs and flows of your own nature and how they respond to your environment."*

As she speaks her light dims further, and you know a third horse has turned black. She smiles, and her light fades completely, enabling you to look at her beauty easily. You glance forward and see the chariot is now pulled by four black horses.

Though it is darker now, it is easier for you to see the ground below and the stars above. You realise that the dreamlike quality of this journey is a reflection of the power of the moon, and see a silver light emanating from Selene again, and one of the horses turn silver.

"One of the greatest gifts I give is intuition, trust yours, for it is always there," Selene informs you.

She leans forward and whispers into your ear, giving you advice on your next steps on the path. You thank her and watch enraptured as she becomes brighter and brighter again, regaining her former radiance. As she does so all the horses turn silver one by one. You know this is an endless cycle, and as you watch her, the white mist appears, filling the chariot around you, until once again you are surrounded by white mist.

Again the mist disperses, and as it fades away you find yourself once more sitting in your room. Take some time to write up your experience and contemplate what you have learned.

THE HORNED GOD

In Ancient Britain and Europe there were many different horned Gods who were worshipped and called upon by our ancestors. Today Wiccans often work with Cernunnos, the ancient Celtic horned God depicted with bull horns or stag's antlers. Cernunnos means *"Horned One"* and it is interesting that it should be Cernunnos who became the predominant modern Horned God, as the majority of ancient reliefs showing horned deities indeed also had bull horns. Bull horns indicated power, which could represent sexual power and/or martial prowess. They emphasise power and fertility and often depictions would show only the head of the God, which was seen as the seat of the soul by the ancient Celtic peoples and was considered to be the most important part of the body to represent in their religious art.

There were also of course many other types of Horned Gods. Some are shown with Ram Horns, some with Goat Horns and some with Stag Antlers. The modern image of Cernunnos has become of Him having stag antlers, despite the original bull horns, due to the identification of the image on the Gundestrup Cauldron with Him. Examination of the Cauldron has shown that it was made in India, and in fact the image on the Gundestrup Cauldron is now thought to be the Indian God Pashupati (Lord of the Beasts), who was an early form of the God Shiva. Goat horns were seen on many of the Horned Gods from ancient Greece and who were introduced throughout the Roman Empire. These Horned Gods include Pan, the *'goatfoot god'*, as well as Faunus and Silvanus. The goat-horned Gods all seem to have a strong affinity with the land and in particular with woodlands and forests and upon their arrival in the British Isles with the Romans they were often equated to some of the local deities.

We can find some inspiration for how the Goat Horned Gods are viewed by modern Wiccans in the writings of Dion Fortune, when she wrote this invocation for the character of Morgan Le Fey, who sings the *"song of the nostalgia of the soul for the vales of Arcady"* to the character of Malcolm, in her novel *Moon Magic*:

"O great god Pan, return to earth again;
Come at my call, and show thyself to men.
Shepherd of goats, upon the wild hill's way,
Forgotten are the ways of sleep and night;

Men seek for them whose eyes have lost the light.
Open the door, the door that hath no key –
The door of dreams whereby men come to thee.
Shepherd of goats, oh answer unto me!" [4]

Stag Antlered Horned Gods were much rarer than the other varieties. Gods depicted with stag antlers were thought to have closeness to nature, as well as being able to grant fertility to the land and animals. Interestingly there are also a few Goddesses who are depicted with Stag Antlers, though we know very little about them today, it is quite possible that their depiction in this way was due to their own associations with fertility and the land. Stag Antlered Gods include Herne and the God Antenocitus (a God indigenous to the British Isles, who was venerated by the Romans). Many modern Pagan books refer to Cernunnos as a stag-horned God, which has led some people to believe that he must be an entirely modern invention. The name *"Cernunnos"* comes from a Gallic image of a God with Bull Horns. The confusion between Bull and Stag-horned may have stemmed from the modern popularity of Herne, a stag-antlered figure associated with Windsor Forest (Berkshire, England) and in more recent times with the *"Robin of Sherwood"* television series. Some modern Pagans have equated Herne to Cernunnos and this may be the root of the confusion (and the popularity!).

Horned Gods were definitely popular throughout ancient history, especially in Britain, but unfortunately there were often no names recorded with the images that we have today and as such we can only make educated guesses by comparing images with names, with the unnamed ones, when it comes to naming them. For this reason, many today prefer to call on the Horned God as *"horned one"* instead of naming him. The classic image of the antlered-horned God shown on

[4] Moon Magic, Dion Fortune

the Gundestrup Cauldron has often incorrectly been associated with Cernunnos. Similar images have been found, dating from early Roman times, in Cirencester (Gloucestershire). Though it is possible that these may be of Antenocitus, the only named Stag-horned God known in Britain; it is more likely that this image relates to the God shown on the Gundestrup Cauldron.

Interestingly though, these images do show the God with two serpents and seated in a half-lotus position, similar to the depiction on the Gundestrup Cauldron! Serpents do make an appearance with other Horned God images too, such as that found in a bronze figure from Wiltshire, showing a horned God holding ram-headed serpents coiling around his legs. The ram-headed serpent is another image strongly linked to Cernunnos!

The ram-headed serpent is particularly associated with the god Cernunnos, and is also seen in the Cirencester relief and the Lypiatt altar, both in Gloucestershire). Interestingly, the ram had strong martial associations, but in the context of the snake it can be seen as emphasising the chthonic wisdom and transformative power associated with the snake.

A number of crude reliefs of a bull-horned god armed with a spear have been found across Britain. These include a naked horned god armed with spear and small globe at Burgh by Sands on the Solway, and a similar figure from Lanchester (Co. Durham). An armed bull-horned god was found in a broken relief at Caernarfon in Wales. Another figure which fits this group was found at Smithfield in London, and shows a horned god bearing a globe and what appears to be a sling or tree branch. The geographical distribution of these figures shows the widespread worship of horned gods in Britain.

As with the feminine divine, it is important to remember that the Horned God or Cernunnos, is not the only way in which the Masculine Divine is viewed in Wicca today. Many other Gods, some of whom are not specifically horned are also called upon, these may include:

★ Hades - the Greek Underworld God and husband of Persephone. Hades is seen as the Dread Lord of Shadows ruling the Underworld.
★ Gwyn Ap Nudd - Welsh Celtic God of the Otherworld Who is also King of the Faeries and Leader of the Wild Hunt.

★ Lugh - the Irish Celtic Lord of Light Who is skilled in all arts and crafts. The festival of Lughnasadh is named after Him.

★ Apollo - the Greek God of Light, Music and Poetry. Apollo was the twin brother of Artemis, and patron of the nine Muses who often accompanied Him.

★ Belenus - the Celtic Solar God also associated with Healing. The festival of Beltane is named after Him.

Exercise 3.2 - Horned God Meditation

Sit comfortably and relax, closing your eyes. In your mind's eye fix the image of yourself sitting as you are in the room. Hold this image, and then see a white mist filling the room, obscuring the walls, the floor, the ceiling, everything, until all around you is white mist. As the mist disperses you find yourself sitting in a grove, with a forest all around you, and the full moon shining down from a starlit sky.

Looking around at the mighty trees towering above you, you see oaks and ashes and hawthorn trees, and hear the rustling of the wind as it blows through their leaves. In the distance you hear an owl hooting, and take this as a signal that you should explore these woods you have found yourself in.

Rising you see there is a path through the trees facing you, leading deeper into the forest. With the light of the full moon casting a silvery glow on the trees and illuminating the way, you follow the path to see where it will lead you. As you walk along the path, the noises of the night forest surround you. You hear the barking of foxes, the hooting of owls, and occasional rustles as small creatures move through the undergrowth.

The noises fade away to be replaced by a crackling sound, and as the smell of wood smoke reaches your nostrils you realise there is a fire burning somewhere ahead of you. You see a reddish-orange glow ahead of you and notice the trees on either side of the path opening out to form a glade. In the centre of the glade is a large bonfire burning, sending sparks high into the night sky. You look around but do not see any signs of life in the glade.

As you gaze at the bonfire burning bright in the centre of the glade,

---

you see a figure forming in its centre. It is a tall man with bull horns
coming out of his head. Around his neck is a large golden torc, and he
is dressed in skins. Coiled around his right arm is a serpent, with ram's
horns coming from its head above its eyes. You know this is
Cernunnos, and as you take in the majesty of his form, he steps out of
the fire to come and stand in front of you.

You bow to Cernunnos, and he smiles to you, holding out his right
hand. You clasp hands with him, and as you do so the serpent slithers
over his hand and around your arm. The dry feel of its scales on your
skin make you feel slightly apprehensive.

Cernunnos says to you, *"The difference between you and the serpent is that
he has grown his horns and understands his nature. When you understand
that you and he are the same, you will understand the mysteries of my realm."*
You look down at the snake, which gazes back at you with a deep look
of understanding that surprises you. Then it slithers back to
Cernunnos and reclaims its place on his arm. Cernunnos smiles again
and says, *"Now you know where my glade is, you can return and visit me at
any time you need to. Remember the mysteries of the horned serpent."* He
turns and walks back into the fire, fading into the flames, and you gaze
after him, calling your thanks.

As you look around the glade again the white mist appears, filling the
air all around you, until once again you are surrounded by white mist.

Again the mist disperses, and as it fades away you find yourself once
more sitting in your room. Take some time to write up your experience
and contemplate what you have learned.

Exercise 3.3 - The Divine

Consider the different views of the divine feminine and masculine, and
decide which one applies to your beliefs. Having decided this, what
do you feel are the most important roles of the Goddess and Horned
God in Wicca? Write this up in your magickal diary, giving examples
of deities that exemplify the different roles.

THE DANCE OF POLARITY

The interplay between the divine masculine and the divine feminine, God and Goddess, is often emphasised in Wicca. This is because Wicca draws on ideas from pre-Christian times for inspiration for their rituals, as well as from a number of other sources. In the pre-Christian cultures the concept of fertility – specifically in this instance meant to refer to the fertility of the land and animals, including humans – was of utmost importance. The mortality rate for infants was high and many did not survive to adulthood. The life expectancy for adults was often only 30 or 40 years, unlike our modern 70-75+! Food could not be bought from supermarkets, if the crops failed, there was no food. If the fertility of domestic or wild animals was low, this would also have an impact on food supplies. There was no alternative, fertility was very important! Today the idea of this fertility is often brought into modern terms relating to fertility of ideas, but it can still be better related maybe to the idea of being able to provide for oneself and ones family. Poverty is still a problem, and not just in the developing world – there are many families who live on the breadline in the West also.

So maybe this is something to consider when you try and equate the idea of fertility to modern concepts, rather than dwelling too much on human or animal fertility, sexual preferences etc. The tradition of Wicca may also have gained some inspiration in regards to the idea of polarity, the interplay between the Goddess and God from a number of other sources.

In Thelema, the philosophical system of magick made popular through the writings of Aleister Crowley and the Ordo Templi Orientis, we find a very clear interplay between the divine feminine and male in the relationship between Nuit and Hadit. Although these Egyptian deities are rarely called upon in Wiccan circles, it is interesting to note that from a Thelemic perspective, Nuit is seen as the all-encompassing Goddess of all, the Goddess of the Night Sky. Hadit is seen as the divine masculine, representing the fertilising point of manifestation within the centre of the circle of existence that is Nuit.

The union of Nuit and Hadit brings forth the conquering child, Ra-Hoor-Khuit, who corresponds to the Wiccan Child of Promise, with similar solar and martial qualities. This is very similar to the idea of the all encompassing Divine Feminine and Divine Masculine, as seen from a henotheistic view in Wicca, through their union they too bring forth the Child of Promise at the rebirth of the Sun at the Winter Solstice!

The concept of union between opposites manifested in male and female Divine also plays a significant role in Qabalah (as practised in the Western Mystery Tradition) and there are many commonalities with the Wiccan views of a Goddess and God. The masculine and feminine divine are both very much emphasised in Qabalah. This may be seen through the titles given to some of the spheres of the Tree of Life, e.g. Binah as the Fertile Mother and Great Mother, Malkuth as the Daughter and Bride, Chokmah as the Great Father, Tiphereth as the Son and Husband, etc.

It may also be seen through the divine names, e.g. Elohim (Gods), which is a female noun with a masculine plural ending, containing both genders within it. Some of the divine names represent the different aspects of the masculine and feminine, e.g. the four letters of the unpronounceable name all relate to the masculine and feminine. So the letters symbolise the divine thus – Yod (Father), Heh (Mother), Vav (Son), Heh (Daughter). The Black and White Pillars, of Severity and Mercy, often referred to in Qabalah, are also attributed to the Goddess and God. Unsurprisingly the Goddess is attributed to the Pillar of Severity! Their balance in the Middle Pillar is considered to be neutral, and does not have a gender-attribution. The Black and White Pillars provided inspiration, possibly through their use in the Hermetic Order of the Golden Dawn, for the placement of the Divine Feminine on the left side of the altar and the Divine Masculine on the right, in Wicca.

Another possible source for the Goddess and God in Wicca is the Harappan culture of the Indus Valley, dating back to before 3000 BCE. This proto-Indian culture worshipped a mother goddess and a horned god (Pashupati), and the image on the Gundestrup Cauldron is now fairly definitely believed to represent him. So the migration of this pairing to Europe could have influenced the development of Celtic worship, and also fit the divine couple of Wicca.

THE TRIPLE GODDESS

Many Wiccan and Pagan groups work with the Divine Feminine in a triple form which is often referred to, not surprisingly, as *'the Triple Goddess'*.

The Triple Goddess is seen by some as Maiden, Mother & Crone. The Maiden Goddess is seen as the bright aspect of the Goddess, the youth, fertility and quite often also virginity. The Mother Goddess is seen as a Goddess of fertility, caring, healing etc. The Crone Goddess represents wisdom and experience as well as the deeper mysteries. Although this concept can work well within a ritual, there seems to be no historical evidence to support the idea that it is an ancient concept. The Triple Goddess as Maiden, Mother & Crone seems to originate from the writings of Robert Graves in his book *The White Goddess* which was first published in 1949. However it is naïve to believe it was all *'invented'* overnight! In 1903 a Cambridge scholar called Jane Ellen Harrison proposed the idea that since ancient times the Goddess had been honoured in three main aspects. She postulated the Maiden, ruling the living, the Mother, ruling the underworld, and an unnamed third aspect.

This idea influenced her colleague James Frazer, who incorporated the *'great goddess'* idea into his classic work *The Golden Bough*, another major influence on modern Wicca. In fact this model also found its way into other writers' works, such as Aleister Crowley, as can be seen in the following quote from his novel *Moonchild*:

> *"Artemis is unassailable, a being fine and radiant; Hecate is the crone, the woman past all hope of motherhood, her soul black with envy and hatred of happier mortals; the woman in the fullness of life is the sublime Persephone."*

There are some Goddesses who are shown in triple forms historically, though they are nearly always portrayed with three faces of the same age. A good example of this is the Goddess Hekate, who is shown in classical art and sculpture as being three younger women, depicted with their backs to each other holding the different tools and symbols which are associated with her mysteries.

It is important to make the distinction between a *'triple goddess'* and the *'Maiden, Mother & Crone'*, as they are not the same thing! There is no historical evidence that a group of goddesses were ever worshipped in the triple function of Maiden, Mother & Crone. Graves, unlike Crowley, was attracted to the concept of the crone goddess. He decided that the Welsh Celtic goddess Ceridwen fitted this mould, and attributed it to her, adding the sow as her animal, a symbol that occurs nowhere in the myths associated with Ceridwen.

Crowley's attributions are not a very coherent set. If you were to apply the model of Maiden, Mother & Crone to the Greek mysteries, there is a much more logical way to do it. Using the Eleusinian Mysteries as the best example, for it explores the mystery of the changing seasons and has three main goddesses in it, a natural attribution arises. Hekate, far from being the crone, would eminently fit the role of Maiden. She is always depicted as a beautiful young maiden, and is never partnered. The  images of her as a crone are later add-ons with no relation to her functions in ancient Greece. Persephone in this myth cycle marries the underworld god Hades, and it is her return each year which brings the fertility of Spring. Therefore Persephone fits admirably into the role of Mother, the one aspect that Crowley gets right! Demeter is the bringer of barren winter through her grief, and is thus the Crone. Although Demeter is a mother, she has become the bringer of desolation, and moved on into the third phase of the model. Thus Hekate, Persephone and Demeter would fit very well into the model of Maiden, Mother &

Crone. In this story the god has two main roles, as Hades the underworld god and Zeus the sky father.

One of the prevalent arguments used to support the idea of the Triple Goddess as Maiden Mother Crone is that these represent the three phases of the Moon. This can work if, in your own work and practises, you ignore the dark phase of the Moon, as the Moon of course has at least four phases – Waxing, Full, Waning and Dark. By simple observation we can see that the lunar month of 28 days naturally divides into four weeks. Some Wiccans also work with the New Moon as the time of new beginnings. There are some who when working with the phases of the Moon compensate for the fourth phase with the concept of a Nymph Goddess, to represent the knowing and sexually active women who has not yet become a mother, making the threefold aspect a fourfold one. This then gives Maiden, Nymph, Mother, and Crone.

It is however important to keep in mind that the Goddess is far more than the Moon. As has already been mentioned she has Stellar and Earthy aspects as well. She is also depicted as the Sun in some pantheons, with the Moon as male. The Solar God and Lunar Goddess idea was prevalent in alchemy in the Middle Ages, which is most probably where Wicca drew its inspiration from.

Examples of Goddesses who are specifically associated with the Sun would include the Egyptian Sekhmet, the Celtic Sulis and Gráinne, and the Japanese Amaterasu. Examples of Moon Gods include the Egyptian Khonsu and Thoth, and the Sumerian Sin.

THE GODS & THE WHEEL OF THE YEAR

Throughout the year, different aspects of the feminine and masculine divine are emphasised at the different *"Wheel of the Year"* Sabbat festivals, emphasising the roles they take during the different seasons of the agricultural and solar year. It is necessary to keep in mind when considering these descriptions, that the individual perception of divinity a practitioner (or group) holds may flavour the way in which these are applied. Furthermore, the way in which two different sets of festivals, those of the early Wiccans (the Major Sabbats) and the Druidic Festivals (Equinoxes & Solstices) were combined, may in places cause confusion / overlap. These issues are again left to the individual (or group) to interpret in their own way.

The Goddess through the Year

★   At Imbolc, the festival of lights, the Goddess is often depicted in aspects like Bride, the healer, and tender of the sacred flame (hence Imbolc being sometimes referred to as Bride).

★   At Eostra, the Goddess is often celebrated as the Goddess of the Dawn and fertility, e.g. Eostra (where the festival name originates) and Ostara.

★   At Beltane the Goddess is seen as the fertile Queen of the Land, full of passion and promise.

★   At Litha (Summer Solstice) the Goddess is the Queen of All, containing life and death within Her in balance.

★   At Lughnasadh the Goddess takes the role of the Reaper, who cuts down the Corn King so that the land and people may prosper in the months to come.

★   At Modron (Autumn Equinox) the role of the Kore (the Maiden), descending to the Underworld to become the Dark Queen is emphasised and as such the mythic stories of

Persephone's abduction and the journey of Inanna to the underworld, are often re-enacted.

★ At Samhain the Goddess is most often seen as the Dark Mother and Queen who is both tomb and womb to the God as He takes his place in the Underworld. Goddesses associated with transformation, such as Ceridwen, the Morrigan and Hekate are often celebrated now.

★ At Yule the role of the Goddess as both the pregnant Mother giving birth to the Solar Child of Promise, as well as the Crone of Winter bleakness (the Cailleach) is emphasised.

The God through the Year

★ At Imbolc the God is represented as the Conquering Child, Sol Invictus, growing in power and starting to turn the tide of winter back.

★ At Eostra He is seen as the Sun Prince, His presence being felt more strongly as more of the plants benefit from His life-giving rays.

★ At Beltane the God grows into His power as the Horned God of the Wildwood, young and horny, chasing the Goddess in order to mate with Her in the ritual of the Sacred Marriage so that the land will be fertilised anew.

★ At Litha the God is seen as the Sun King in His prime, yet within this is the promise of death to come, for after the Summer Solstice powers start to decline.

★ At Lughnasadh the God is celebrated as the Corn King, cut down (sacrificed) so that the people may live, feeding on His body as ale and bread made from the harvest.

★ At Modron the God is seen as the Lord of the Vine, dancing His last dance on the Earth before He descends to the Underworld for the winter months.

★ At Samhain the God is celebrated as the Lord of Death, Dread Lord of Shadows and Lord of the Underworld. He is now seen as the Comforter who brings with Him a promise of Life to come.

★ At Yule the cycle is completed and the God is reborn as the Child of Promise, the Solar Child. Though weak, He grows stronger through the year.

Exercise 3.4 – The God, Goddess & Sabbats

Write the different phases of the Goddess and God at each of the Sabbat festivals of the Wheel of the Year in your magickal diary. If you are artistic, you might consider creating a wheel drawing writing in and drawing the different faces and symbolisms.

Key Points

★ There is no set viewpoint on the divine in Wicca, it is a personal perception based on your experiences and views.

★ However the Goddess is usually seen as being lunar, and also represents the stars and the earth.

★ The Horned God is usually seen as solar, and also representing the underworld and life in nature.

★ Many groups and individuals work with the Goddess in a triple form.

★ The Goddess and God are seen in different ways at the Sabbats through the year.

Further Optional Reading:

★ *Hekate: Keys to the Crossroads* edited by Sorita d'Este with various contributors.

★ *Horns of Power: Manifestations of the Horned God* edited by Sorita d'Este with various contributors.

★ *The Witches God* by Janet and Stewart Farrar

★ *The Witches' Goddess* by Janet and Stewart Farrar

LESSON 4

THE FOUR ELEMENTS

Wiccans work with the four elements, Air, Fire, Water and Earth. The elements make up everything in the world around us; they are concepts, energy states, states of being and philosophical concepts. They are fundamental to our existence. By working with the elements we enable ourselves to be balanced and remain centred, whilst at the same time promoting personal growth through realization of imbalances within ourselves. These imbalances may be personality traits, emotions or negative habits and by working with the four elements we can transmute and change them into positive qualities.

The philosophy of the four elements originates with the ancient Greek philosopher Empedocles, who formulated the idea in the fifth century BCE and elaborated on it in his work *Tetrasomia* (*"Doctrine of the Four Elements"*). Empedocles expressed the idea that the four elements were not only the physical building blocks of the material universe, but also spiritual essences.

Since the time of Empedocles the four elements have played a major part in the development of magick, and can be found in all the magickal traditions which influenced the development of Wicca. It is a tribute to the lucidity of Empedocles' philosophy that this idea is still used today in much the same form as he described.

THE ELEMENT OF AIR

Air is the breath of life. We are surrounded by the Air, invisible yet always present. Air is the subtlest of the four elements, intangible and connecting us to the stars, as the atmosphere which fills the gap between the Earth and the heavens. Air represents the intellect, the power of thought and knowledge. With knowledge comes the power of communication to transmit knowledge, best expressed through the words we speak, which travel through the air.

Air is associated with inspiration, a term which can literally mean *"to breathe in"*. When we are inspired ideas move in our minds, and movement is a quality of air, as seen in nature by the power of the wind, which varies from a gentle breeze to a raging tornado. Air is also associated with joy and happiness, the lightness of spirit you feel when you are in a good mood. Feeling happy is often described as *"floating on air"*.

Air - "To Know"

Tools	Wand, White-handled Knife, Censer
Direction	East
Time	Dawn
Season	Spring
Colours	Yellow, White
Sense	Smell
Concepts	Clarity, Discrimination, Intellect, Intuition, Knowledge, Mind, Sound, Speed
Qualities (+)	Analysis, Decisiveness, Discernment, Happiness, Hope, Joy, Logic, Inspiration, Wisdom
Qualities (-)	Anxiety, Fear, Dispersion, Impulsiveness, Insecurity, Paranoia, Prejudice

Exercise 4.1 - Air Meditation

Inhale to a count of four, holding the breath to a count of four, and then exhaling to a count of four. This technique will accustom you to regulating your breath. With practice it becomes automatic so you do not have to concentrate on your breath when meditating, and you can control your breath automatically whilst meditating using another focus.

For relaxation inhale to a count of four and exhale to a count of eight. This can be increased with practice, but the exhalation should always be longer than the inhalation, preferably double the length.

THE ELEMENT OF FIRE

Fire is the great transformer. Fire is the least obviously present around us of the four elements. It is the next most subtle of the elements after Air, it flickers and dances, leaping up to die down and be gone again. Fire can be creative or destructive, and this is clearly seen in nature. A forest fire may 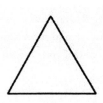 initially seem devastating, but many plants actually need fire in their life cycle to ensure their continued survival, a fact that research has made clear in recent years. Fire burns, and reminds us of the importance of control. When handled properly Fire provides light and heat, and can be used to cook. If Fire is allowed to get out of control it can cause great destruction. In the same way Fire represents our will and our passions. If controlled they can be creative and constructive, enabling us to develop and do great things. But if we let them get out of control we can become obsessive, or violent. Through the light of Fire we can see our path, enabling the process of transformation that it facilitates to continue.

Fire -"To Will"

Tools	Athame
Direction	South
Time	Noon
Season	Summer
Colours	Reds, Oranges
Sense	Sight
Concepts	Drive, Energy, Freedom, Light, Power, Success, Transmutation, Vision
Qualities (+)	Courage, Creativity, Drive, Enthusiasm, Motivation, Passion, Will
Qualities (-)	Cruelty, Egotism, Fickleness, Possessiveness, Vengefulness, Violence

Exercise 4.2 - Fire Meditation

This meditation can be done with any normal candle. The candle should be placed at least a metre (just over three foot) from the wall, there should be no other light source in the room, and the curtains should be drawn. Focus your gaze on the flame of the candle. Spend a few minutes simply watching the flame, how it dances, growing and diminishing. Notice the play of different colours in the flame, the inner blue around the wick and the fiery shades or red, orange, and yellow.

Make a note of how this made you feel. Many people find this meditation a good one to calm and focus their mind, and use it for this purpose before performing rituals or other meditations.

THE ELEMENT OF WATER

Life began in the waters. Water is vital for life, and like Fire it can be both nurturing and destructive. In nature water is all around us as rain, rivers, lakes and oceans. The seas move in tides, and this reflects our motions, which ebb and flow like those tides. Water can represent both serenity, like  the still surface of a lake, or sexual energy and love, which can be as changeable and overwhelming as the sea. Like Air, Water transports things, and this is reflected in the associated sense of taste, which tells us whether we want to eat or drink something. Water can be overwhelming, reflecting extremes, from the nurturing it provides to death when it is in its extreme forms.

Water -"To Dare"

Tools	Chalice
Direction	West
Time	Dusk
Season	Autumn
Colours	Blues
Sense	Taste
Concepts	Blood, Death/Rebirth, Dreams, Emotions, Intuition, Primal Chaos, Taste, Underworld, Womb
Qualities (+)	Compassion, Depth, Empathy, Nurture, Serenity, Sexuality, Sympathy, Tranquillity, Trust
Qualities (-)	Deceit, Hatred, Insipid, Jealousy, Sadness, Sorrow, Spite, Treachery, Venom

Exercise 4.3 - Water Meditation

For this meditation you need a bowl of water and an ice cube. Place the bowl on the floor and sit comfortably gazing into it. Add the ice cube and watch it float around on the surface as it slowly melts. Consider how it moves and changes state, from solid to liquid, and contemplate the power of water in nature all around you, and how it exists as solid (ice), liquid (water) and gas (water vapour). Spend a few minutes doing this, or until the ice cube melts. Record your thoughts and observations.

THE ELEMENT OF EARTH

Earth gives us the solidity of the physical realm which we inhabit. Earth is the most solid of the elements, and hence it has associated qualities like endurance, patience, strength, tolerance and steadfastness. Earth is also associated with sensuality, reflected in the pleasures of physical activity. The sense of touch is associated with earth, we say we are *"in touch"* with someone when we keep a link between us. Earth is also a nurturing element, providing the food we eat, and making up the materials used to build houses, and indeed being the ground beneath our feet. Earth teaches us that through dedication, patience and toil, all things are possible.

Earth - "To Keep Silent"

Tools	Pentacle
Direction	North
Time	Midnight
Season	Winter
Colours	Greens & Browns
Sense	Touch
Concepts	Body, Endurance, Healing, Mystery, Power, Skill, Strength, Stillness, Touch
Qualities (+)	Humility, Patience, Persistence, Realization, Responsibility, Selflessness, Sensuality, Stability, Steadfastness, Strength, Tolerance
Qualities (-)	Attention-Seeking, Depression, Domineering, Greed, Inertia, Laziness, Melancholy, Stubbornness

Exercise 4.4 - Earth Meditation

For this meditation you need a small bowl of earth.[5] Sit comfortably with the bowl of earth on the floor in front of you. Lift the bowl to your face and smell its deep earthy fragrance. Then hold the bowl in one hand and put your other hand in the earth. Close your eyes and feel the texture of the earth in your hand, feel its nurturing power and be aware of the variety of life that grows in earth. How does the earth make you feel? What images and memories come to mind? Spend a few minutes exploring these feelings and then make a note of how you feel.

5 This should be Earth from your garden or otherwise natural and fertile – not sand!

Exercise 4.5 - Elemental Body Meditation

Contemplate in turn the effect of the elements and their presence within your body. Start with Air, and concentrate on the breath entering and leaving your body. Focus on how oxygen is transported in your blood all around your body, how carbon dioxide is transported to your lungs to be exhaled, and all the spaces in your body that are occupied by Air, such as in your mouth, ears, lungs, etc. Next concentrate on the element of Fire within yourself. Feel the fire of digestion in your stomach, as food is broken down and turned into fuel for the body. Feel the fire of electricity as messages are sent along your nerves, synapses sparking and passing on all the signals that keep your body functioning, the thoughts in your mind. Move on to the element of Water within your body. Think of the water in your saliva, in your eyes, the moisture within you. Then consider all the water in your blood and other fluids, and the water that makes up the bulk of your tissues in your body, for you are mostly made of Water. Now consider the element of Earth within you, the solidity of your bones and nails, your hair and teeth, your skin. Think how Earth gives you form and defines the shape you are. When you have done this for a while consider how all the elements work in harmony to create the temple of your body.

Exercise 4.6 - Correspondences

Write all the attributions for the four elements into your magickal diary. Remember to add their elemental symbols with your entries so that you have this for future reference should you need it.

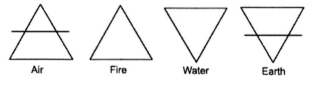

| Air | Fire | Water | Earth |

THE ELEMENTAL GUARDIANS

In ceremonies the Elemental Guardians, or 'Watchtowers' are invoked at each of the cardinal points of the circle. The attributions are as follow:

★ Air – East
★ Fire - South
★ Water - West
★ Earth – North

These attributions, as they appear in Wicca, originate from the writings of the nineteenth century French occultist Eliphas Levi, much of whose work was used by the Hermetic Order of the Hermetic Order of the Golden Dawn. These attributions were incorporated into a ceremony called the Lesser Banishing Ritual of the Pentagram (LBRP) which was created by members of the Hermetic Order of the Golden Dawn in the late 1800's. The use of the elements in this way is not something which is found in earlier Witchcraft (pre-Gardnerian) traditions. The elements, as used in Wicca, also each have a colour attributed to it, again drawn from the LBRP, these are:

★ Air – Yellow
★ Fire - Red
★ Water - Blue
★ Earth – Green

The Elemental Guardians are called on for two purposes in Wiccan ceremonies. They are called to act as guardians of the sacred space, or to bring their energy and associated qualities into the circle, or both. As guardians they stand at the cardinal points of the circle keeping any unwanted influences out of your circle. When they are called to bring their energies into the circle, they are acting as lenses to focus the elemental energy into your circle so you can draw on it to empower your rites.

TO KNOW, TO WILL,

TO DARE, TO KEEP SILENT

The magickal axiom of *"To know, To Will, To Dare and To Keep Silent"* is one that is worth consideration by those wishing to practice any form of magick successfully. It can be found in the writings of the occultist Eliphas Levi:

"Four phrases constitute and include all that is required for the possession of High Magical Power.
To Know; To Dare; To Will; To Keep Silent."[6]

Each of the phrases can be attributed to one of the four elements as they correspond perfectly to the concepts associated with each. They are attributed as follows:

- ★ To Know – The Element of Air
- ★ To Will – The Element of Fire
- ★ To Dare – The Element of Water
- ★ To Keep Silent – The Element of Earth

Each of these phrases embodies concepts which are vital to successful magick and spiritual growth. You need knowledge (To Know) to be able to make informed choices, and the more you learn the clearer your choices become. You need willpower (To Will) to power your intent and have the strength of purpose to remain fixed on your goals and achieve them without being swayed from your purpose. You need daring (To Dare) to have the courage of your convictions to be true to yourself and your ideals and ethics without letting others influence you. You need silence (To Keep Silent) to know when it is better to not disclose information or ideas, when it might harm others to know, or when you do not want to dissipate the energy

---

[6] Transcendental Magic by Eliphas Levi

put into a spell, or when you are meditating and finding harmony within.

Exercise 4.7 - Strengths & Weaknesses

Which of the four axioms do you feel is strongest in you?
Write the whole phrase in your magickal diary, and assess your strengths and weaknesses in each of the four areas.

Key Points

★ Wiccans work with the four elements of Air, Fire, Water and Earth.

★ Each element has a range of correspondences which form the basis for much of the ritual practice in Wicca.

★ Elemental guardians are called to guard the magick circle and to contribute elemental energy to ceremonies.

Further Suggested Reading

★ *Practical Elemental Magick* by David Rankine and Sorita d'Este
★ *Transcendental Magic* by Eliphas Levi

LESSON 5

THE TIMES OF MAGICK

A ritual or ceremony should always have a purpose, as ritual for the sake of ritual will soon become pointless. In the Wiccan tradition many of our rituals are performed at particular times marked by the natural cycles of the Earth, Sun and Moon. Wiccans further believe that certain times are better for performing certain types of magickal ceremonies than others. This belief that particular times are better for magick, or associated with particular types of magick has long been held by magickians throughout the ages.

In ancient Egypt, for example, magick was always performed during the daylight hours, with dawn and midday seen as the best time to work it. Additionally there were *"good"* and *"bad"* days for doing magick on. The Egyptians were not the only ones to do this, the Greeks, Romans and pretty much every other civilization had times which were special to them. The magickians of the Middle Ages and Renaissance who wrote down their rituals would often perform their ceremonies at the most auspicious phase of the Moon, at particular points of the Solar year or according to a system of planetary hours attributed to each day.

When looking at the natural world we can clearly see the origins of some of these beliefs. After all plants grow with more vigour in the Spring and Summer, the landscape is often bleak in Winter. Autumn is a time of change, as is Spring. Likewise there are widespread beliefs that plant growth can also be linked to the phases of the Moon, growing more strongly during the waxing Moon, less so during the waning Moon and that certain lunar phases are better for planting certain crops at. The Equinoxes are times of balance, light and dark are balanced, therefore the energies of the world around us are more likely to be in harmony also.

We will now consider in more detail times which are of particular interest for those wishing to perform Wiccan ceremonies and magick. We will look at the *'Wheel of the Year'* the eight seasonal festivals which are generally celebrated by Wiccans of all traditions, as well as the Full Moon celebrations which are sometimes referred to as Esbats. In addition to these we will also consider other times which may be useful to take into consideration when performing magickal ceremonies and which, although part of some Wiccan traditions, often less known than the Sabbats and Esbats.

THE WHEEL OF THE YEAR

Wiccans celebrate the cyclic nature of the Earth through the celebration of the seasonal festivals, there are eight of these festivals which are often referred to as *'The Wheel of the Year'* forming a wheel with eight spokes equally spaced. These festivals are known as Sabbats and are celebrated at key turning points in the seasons throughout each solar year.

By celebrating the festivals you attune yourself to the cycles of nature, both within yourself and in the world around you. The eight-fold concept of *'The Wheel of the Year'* is a modern concept, inasmuch as no one group of people in the ancient world would have celebrated these festivals in the way Wiccans and other modern Pagan groups do today. Additionally, it is worth keeping in mind that although the way in which the festivals are combined today is a relatively new concept, there is also absolutely no doubt that all the festivals on the Wheel of the Year are rooted in British and European history. We would recommend that you read the excellent book *Stations of the Sun* by Prof. Ronald Hutton if you are interested in finding out more about the various historic festivals which took place throughout the year in Britain, often corresponding to the festivals which are celebrated by Wiccans today.

The Wheel of the Year turns each solar year and returns to the same festival, but as with all things in the Natural world it will never be exactly the same. The cyclic nature of the seasons has been with us since the beginnings of history and will be with us until the very end of time. Though global warming and shifts in weather patterns may change the tides of the seasons, the seasons themselves will not stop. It spirals from and to eternity, with new discoveries and wisdom to be gained from each cycle.

Early followers of Gerald Gardner's Wicca only celebrated what is now known as the *'Major Sabbats'* these are:

★ Imbolc (Bride)
★ Beltane (Roodmas)
★ Lughnasadh (Lammas)
★ Samhain (All-Hallows)

Around the same time, the Druid revivalists who worked with Ross Nichols, only celebrated the Equinoxes and Solstices, which was subsequently incorporated by Gerald Gardner and his initiates. These are known in Wicca today as the *'Lesser Sabbats'*:

★ Spring Equinox (Ostara)
★ Summer Solstice (Litha)
★ Autumn Solstice (Modron)
★ Winter Solstice (Yule)

Samhain (Halloween) – 31st October

Samhain, or Halloween, is the death festival, marking the descent of Winter, when the Summer goes to its rest. The leaves are falling from the trees in drifts, and life draws away from the surface of the earth, descending deep into the earth into the roots and bulbs of plants which rest over the Winter. Although there are no wild flowers blooming, the colours of nature are still rich and warm. Samhain is the third harvest festival, the harvest of flesh. The livestock would have been killed at this time so that there would be meat throughout the bleak Winter. Samhain is a time of transformation and inner work. It is also a sombre time of remembrance, when we remember and honour those who have died. The veil is thinnest between the worlds and we call on the spirits of the dead and invite them to feast with us on this, the feast of death. We call upon our ancestors and contact the ancient wisdom. It is a time of endings, but also of beginnings, as Samhain is a Celtic New Year's Eve festival. Thus we give up the past and look to the future, and with this in mind it is also a good time for performing divinations – in particular skrying into flames, water, mirrors or crystals are appropriate workings for this festival.

Winter Solstice (Yule) – 21st December

At Yule we say goodbye to the dying Sun, and wait through the long, cold night for the Sun's rebirth as the Child of Promise. The rising Sun brings the promise of the spring and the gifts that will bring. It is still a long time before the Sun will be strong, but we hope and we trust. Yule is a turning point, a point of change, where the tides of the year turn and begin to flow in the opposite direction. It is the darkest time of the year, the time of the longest night, but there is the promise of the return of lighter and warmer times.

To light the long night people would burn the Yule log. The Yule log would be the last log brought into the home, which would be kept for the next year to begin the Yule fire, until it had burned away and was replaced by another one. As many homes no longer have a hearth fire and it may not be practical to have a fire in an indoors ceremony Wiccans often make a symbolic Yule log for use in ceremonies. This takes the form of a decorated log, with a candle for each person present. The candles are lit by each person in turn as they make a wish for the year to come, thinking of hopes for the coming year, and of setting resolutions. From the darkness comes light.

Imbolc (Bride) – 1st February

The Festival of Imbolc is celebrated on 1st February, and was referred to as *"Imbolc, when the ewes are milked at Spring's beginning."* Imbolc is Irish-Gaelic, translated variously as *"in the belly"* and *"ewe's milk"*. The first stirrings of Spring can be seen as the first flowers like snowdrops and winter aconite begin to appear. Seeds which have lain dormant within the Earth begin to stir with life, as yet unseen.

In Wicca it is the traditional time for initiation. Now is the time for the banishing of Winter and the welcoming of Spring. The last grain from the Harvest Festival was ritually brought into the house at Imbolc, blessed and planted as the first seed of the next harvest.

Spring Equinox (Eostre) –22nd March

This festival is named after the Anglo-Saxon Goddess Eostre, also known in Old German as Ostara. Little is known about this Goddess, except that Her festival was celebrated at the Spring Equinox. The Anglo-Saxon lunar month which became April, was called Easter-monath. The equinox is a time both of fertility and new life, and of balance and harmony. Light and dark are here in balance, but the light is growing stronger. It is a time of birth, and of manifestation. Daffodils, tulips and crocuses are all in full bloom, blossom appears on trees and catkins can be found on the hazel and willow. The days grow lighter and the earth grows warmer. This is a time both of growth and of balance, and we may work on balancing ourselves and the subtle energies within us, such as the inner masculine and feminine qualities, the light and dark aspects, etc. This is the time of spring's return, the joyful time, the seed time, when life bursts forth from the earth and the chains of winter are broken.

Beltane (Roodmas) – 1st May

Beltane from the Irish Gaelic, *"Bealtaine"*, means *"Bel Fire"*, taking its name from the fires that were lit at this time of year for the Sun God Belenus. Like Samhain, it is a time when the veil is thin between the worlds, a time to communicate with spirits, particularly nature spirits and faerie. Beltane is a time of fertility and is also an excellent time for Handfastings, the couple enacting the *Heiros gamos*, or sacred marriage of the Divine Feminine and Divine Masculine. Fires were traditionally built at Beltane, and people would jump over the fire for luck or blessings. Young, unmarried people would leap the bonfire and wish for a husband or wife, young women would leap it to ensure their fertility and couples leap it to strengthen a bond. Cattle were driven through the ashes or between two Beltane fires to ensure a good milk yield.

Summer Solstice (Litha) –21st of June

At the Summer Solstice the sun is at its highest and brightest and the day at its longest. The Summer Solstice is a time of fulfilment of love. June was considered by some to be the luckiest month to be married in, and is the time of the mead moon, or honey moon. A tradition was for newly weds to drink mead daily for a month after their wedding, hence the post wedding holiday being named the honeymoon. This is a time of beauty, love, strength, energy, rejoicing in the warmth of the sun, and the promise of the fruitfulness to come. It seems a carefree time, yet in the knowledge of life, is the knowledge of death, and beauty is but transitory. We celebrate life, and the triumph of light, but acknowledge death, and the power of the dark which now begins to grow stronger.

Lughnasadh (Lammas) - 1st August

Lughnasadh or Lammas is celebrated on August eve or August 1st and is the festival of the first of the harvests, the grain harvest. Lammas is the Anglo-Saxon name for the festival, meaning *"Loaf mass"*. Lammas is a time of the fullness of Life, and a celebration of the bountiful earth. It is a time of the sacrificial mating of Goddess and God, where the Corn King, given life by the Goddess and tasting of her love is sacrificed and transformed into bread and ale which feeds us. The main themes of Lammas may therefore be seen as thanksgiving to the Gods their bountiful harvest, stating our hopes for what we wish to harvest (for Lammas is the very beginning of the harvest), sacrifice, and transformation.

Autumn Equinox (Modron) –21st of September

The two equinoxes are times of equilibrium. Day and night are equal and the tide of the year flows steadily, but whilst the Spring

Equinox manifests the equilibrium before action, the Autumnal Equinox represents the repose after action, the time to take satisfaction in the work of the summer and reap its benefits. It takes its name of Modron from the Welsh goddess, whose name means *"Mother"*. The Autumnal Equinox is celebrated around the 21st September, and is the second harvest festival, with the fruit being gathered in. We celebrate the abundance of the earth, and make wine from the excess fruit, to preserve the richness of the fruits of the earth to give us joy throughout the year.

Please note

The dates given above festivals are for the Northern Hemisphere. The seasons in the Southern Hemisphere are reversed. There are much debate about whether the festivals should also be reversed, kept the same or indeed adapted to local environmental conditions, indigenous festivals and climate. If you live in the Southern Hemisphere this is something for you to contemplate and decide for yourself, it might be best starting by simply reversing the festival dates (i.e. Move them on by six months) and work through a cycle of festivals in order to get a feel for what works. There are no hard and fast rules here, though it might be useful finding Wiccan groups in your area and speaking to the members about what they do.

In both the Southern and Northern Hemispheres the dates for Equinoxes and Solstices may vary from year to year, so it is important to consult an astrological calendar for the exact dates each year.

In some parts of the world (Northern or Southern Hemisphere), it may be necessary to adapt the festivals completely, due to the difference in the demarcation of the seasons, as such it will be necessary to observe both carefully the changes in nature, as well as research the local festivals for important agricultural dates. For example: Lammas is the grain harvest festival – when are the grain crops being harvested in the country you live?

Exercise 5.1 - Wheel of the Year Meditation

Sit comfortably and relax, closing your eyes. In your mind's eye fix the image of yourself sitting as you are in the room. Hold this image, and then see a white mist filling the room, obscuring the walls, the floor, the ceiling, everything, until all around you is white mist. As the mist disperses you find yourself sitting in a field, with a wood about thirty metres in front of you.

As you look around you see snow on the ground, and in the trees, blanketing the landscape with white. Studying your surroundings, you notice spots of colour in the snow, and see the yellow flowers of crocuses, poking out of the snow towards the sun.

A closer look also shows you the white flowers of winter aconite, revealed by their green stalks. The air is crisp and cool with the last biting winds of winter, and the sun shines brightly low in the morning sky, hinting at the pleasures of spring to come.

As the day starts the snow melts, and more flowers spring up from the ground. You see the yellow daffodils and red tulips, and in the trees the green foliage of fresh leaves, with the catkins starting to blossom on the hazel and willow trees. The day grows warmer and there is a sense of balance in the air around you. As you look around you see hares bounding through the fields, and stopping occasionally to box each other.

The day continues to grow warmer, and now you see white blossoms on some of the trees ahead of you, as the hawthorn comes into blossom. You hear a bellow and a clattering sound, and turn around to see two stags butting horns in the distance.

Behind them the herd waits to see who will rule and mate with the does. As the sap rises and the quickening energy fills nature, you feel yourself becoming more alert and active.

The sun reaches its peak overhead and the sun is now beating down on you. Flowers are blooming all around you, and the air is filled with the buzzing of bees collecting pollen. The colour in the field is matched by the colour in the air as butterflies flutter around you. Life is everywhere at its peak, and you feel completely alive and full of vigour.

The sun starts to move from its zenith, and the air grows almost imperceptibly less warm. You look to the right and see a field of corn growing there, ripe for the harvest. Patches of red amongst the golden yellow shows where poppies are in full flower. Figures move in the field, wielding scythes and cutting the corn down to be baled and stored. Birds fly overhead waiting to land and peck at the remaining grains on the earth.

Evening is approaching, and as you look at the woods you see the leaves are starting to turn shades of brown and yellow. In the bushes you can make out spots of red and black colour amidst the green, and know the berries are ripening for the fruit harvest. Swallows and other small birds can be seen in the sky migrating to warmer climates.

The sun is setting below the horizon and it is dusk. The air is getting colder and the leaves are falling from the trees. Most of the flowers have died and their bulbs go into hibernation for the winter. Overhead the honking of geese announces the return of these winter visitors, and you can just make out their V formations against the evening sky.

Now it is night, and the landscape is illuminated by the moon. All the trees are bare, apart from a few evergreens. The fields and bushes look stark and barren with the absence of leaves and growing plants. Only the ever-present grass assures you there is still life in the earth beneath you. You know the sunrise will bring the first signs of spring again. As you look around the white mist appears, filling the air around you, until once again you are surrounded by white mist. Again the mist disperses, and as it fades away you find yourself once more sitting in your room. Take some time to write up your experience and contemplate what you have learned.

Consider particularly which part of the meditation you felt most in tune with, and why this may have been. What does it tell you about yourself?

THE TIDES OF THE MOON

"When I shall have departed from this world,
Whenever ye have need of anything,
Once in the month, and when the moon is full,
Ye shall assemble in some desert place,
Or in a forest all together join
To adore the potent spirit of your queen,
My mother, great Diana..."[7]

Whether you live in the city or in a rural area, a clear starlit night adorned with the light of the Full Moon is one of the most beautiful sights our human eyes can behold. For many the Moon still holds a great deal of mystery and power, just like it did in earlier times. In times gone by, the Moon was considered to be a mysterious land which was inhabited by the Gods, a place where our souls journeyed to upon death. In many ancient civilisations it was thought that the universe revolved around the Earth and the Moon was seen as the closest of the celestial bodies, occupying the first orbit around the Earth.

Early man understood that the changing faces of the Moon affected them, as the Moon waxed and waned, it influenced the tides of the waters on Earth and the growth of plants. Today we know that the Moon does indeed revolve around the Earth, but also of course that the Earth, together with the other planets revolves around the Sun in a continuous cycle. The movement of the Earth around the Sun brings with it the changing seasons.

In addition to working with the cycles of the seasons, Wiccans and Pagan Witches also work with the cyclic phases of the Moon, drawing on its mystical powers and energies, and timing our rituals and magickal workings accordingly.

---

[7] The Aradia, Gospel of the Witches by Charles Leland, 1899

Moon Phase	Description	Types of Magick
New Moon	The first sliver of light becomes visible after a dark moon, appearing as faint crescent	This is a good time to do workings for new projects, or to perform magick for new beginnings.
Waxing Moon	This is the period during which the Moon appears to grow in light, slowly with each passing day towards being full.	This is an excellent time for doing magickal work for increase, including wealth, better health and growth.
Full Moon	The entire illuminated side of the Moon faces towards the Earth and the Moon appears in the night sky as a large and bright disk.	Most Wiccan magick is performed when the Moon is full as it is an ideal time for bringing things into fruition.
Waning Moon	This is the period during which the light of the Moon appears to slowly shrink with each passing day towards the time when it completely disappears.	This is a good time for doing magick towards decrease.
Dark Moon	This is the period during which the Moon appears invisible and reflects no light back towards the Earth.	The Dark Moon is a good time for performing magickal workings aimed at introspection, as well as for performing workings to banish negativity.

Exercise 5.2 -Lunar Phases

Copy the lunar phases and their associated types of magick into your magickal diary.

DAYS OF THE WEEK

Since ancient Greece the days of the week have been attributed to the seven classical planets. Although the Sun and Moon are not planets, they were considered as such by the ancients, together with Mercury, Venus, Mars, Jupiter and Saturn. These seven celestial bodies were the ones which were seen to move in the sky, and were known as the *"wandering stars"* or *"deathless powers"*. The names we use for the days of the week are taken from Roman and Saxon deities:

Day of the Week	Planet	Named After
Sunday	The Sun	Sol, The Sun (Roman)
Monday	The Moon	Luna, The Moon (Roman)
Tuesday	Mars	Tiw (Saxon)
Wednesday	Mercury	Woden (Saxon)
Thursday	Jupiter	Thunor / Thor (Saxon)
Friday	Venus	Frigga (Saxon)
Saturday	Saturn	Saturn (Roman)

The planetary attributions we use today for the days are exactly the same as those used in ancient Greece. Each of the days, with its associated planet, is connected with different types of magickal work, as illustrated below:

Day	Planet	Type of Magick
Sunday	The Sun	Career success, establishing harmony, healing, improving health, developing leadership skills, acquiring wealth, gaining promotion, strengthening willpower and energy.
Monday	The Moon	Clairvoyance, Safe Childbirth, Divination of the future, developing glamour and illusions, protection for travelling by sea
Tuesday	Mars	Control of Anger, increasing courage, energy and passion, increasing sex drive, vigour
Wednesday	Mercury	Business success, communication skills, knowledge, memory, diplomacy, exam success, divination, developing influence, protection for travel by air and land, learning music.

Thursday	Jupiter	Career success, developing ambition and enthusiasm, improving health, wealth, acquiring honour, improving humour, legal matters, leadership and luck
Friday	Venus	Increasing attractiveness, beauty and passion. Enhancing creativity, improving fertility, friendships, obtaining love and increasing self-confidence.
Saturday	Saturn	Performing duty, establish balance, studying for exams, dispelling illusions, protecting the home, dealing with legal matters, developing patience and self-discipline.

The exercises which follow are from our book *Practical Planetary Magick*[8] and are designed to help develop a stronger understanding of the planetary energies, the symbols associated with each of the planets and the energies associated with each of the planets. We have included them here as we personally feel that the importance of the planets, the deities associated with the planets and their respective correspondences are such an important part of modern magickal practice that they will benefit students who are eager to develop their practical skills and their understanding of western magick a bit more at this time.

---

[8] Practical Planetary Magick by Sorita d'Este and David Rankine, Avalonia, 2007

PLANETARY CONTEMPLATIONS

Although there are sometimes variations of these symbols in use, the symbols given for each of the seven classical planets with each of the exercises that follow, are those which are used as standard today.

The Sun

Close your eyes and visualise the Sun symbol in gold on a purple background. As you visualise the golden circle with its central golden dot, contemplate the solar qualities of egotism, friendship, joy, success, wealth and will. How strong are each of these forces in your life? Which of them are you actively trying to cultivate or transform? What other qualities or events do they bring to mind as you contemplate their influences?

Mercury

Close your eyes and visualise the Mercury symbol in orange on a blue background. As you visualise the orange circle on top of the orange equal-armed cross, surmounted by the orange crescent with its horns up, contemplate the Mercurial qualities of communication, deception, flexibility, magick, memory and speed. How strong are each of these forces in your life? Which of them are you actively trying to cultivate or transform? What other qualities or events do they bring to mind as you contemplate their influences?

Venus

Close your eyes and visualise the Venus symbol in green on a red background. As you visualise the emerald green circle on top of the emerald green equal-armed cross, contemplate the Venusian qualities of beauty, culture, fertility, love, sexuality and sociability. How strong are each of these forces in your life? Which of them are you actively trying to cultivate or transform? What other qualities or events do they bring to mind as you contemplate their influences?

Moon

Close your eyes and visualise the Moon symbol in silver on a yellow background. As you visualise the silver crescent facing to the left, contemplate the Lunar qualities of clairvoyance, dreams, glamour, spirituality, transformation, and your unconscious.
How strong are each of these forces in your life? Which of them are you actively trying to cultivate or transform? What other qualities or events do they bring to mind as you contemplate their influences?

Mars

Close your eyes and visualise the Mars symbol in red on a green background. As you visualise the scarlet red circle with the scarlet red arrow coming out of the upper right (NE) of the circle, contemplate the Martial qualities of anger, courage, passion, strength, vengeance and vigour. How strong are each of these forces in your life? Which of them are you actively trying to cultivate or transform? What other qualities or events do they bring to mind as you contemplate their influences?

Jupiter

Close your eyes and visualise the Jupiter symbol in blue on an orange background. As you visualise the sapphire blue equal-armed cross with the sapphire blue crescent facing left joined to the leftmost tip of the horizontal bar of the cross, contemplate the Jupiterian qualities of authority, ethics, fortune, humour, responsibility and truth. How strong are each of these forces in your life? Which of them are you actively trying to cultivate or transform? What other qualities or events do they bring to mind as you contemplate their influences?

Saturn

Close your eyes and visualise the Saturn symbol in black on a white background. As you visualise the black equal-armed cross with the black left-facing crescent attached to the bottom of the cross, contemplate the Saturnian qualities of austerity, duty, equilibrium, limitation, patience and self-discipline. How strong are each of these forces in your life? Which of them are you actively trying to cultivate or transform? What other qualities or events do they bring to mind as you contemplate their influences?

Exercise 5.2 - Your Planet

Which of the contemplations had the biggest effect on you?
Was it the one you expected?
If not, why do you think this was the case?

ELEMENTAL TIMES

As you have already seen in lesson 4, there are times associated with the elements as well as the planets. Both the day and the year are also divided into four elemental segments. The elemental tides of the year are also known as the four seasons! The divisions of the day are based more on the movement of the Sun, and so are far more likely to be unequal segments than four exact quarters.

Element	Season	Time of Day	Harmonious Planets
Air	Spring	Dawn	Mercury
Fire	Summer	Midday	Mars, Sun
Water	Autumn	Dusk	Moon, Jupiter
Earth	Winter	Midnight	Venus, Saturn

The Elemental times tie in strongly with types of magick, and can be used to add an extra layer of symbolism and focus to spells and ceremonies. If you choose to, you can work with the elemental tides and the lunar tides, as they work very well together. The Elemental times also work well with the planetary energies, particularly if you take into account the type of elemental energy which is strongest in the planets. This principle of reinforcement is one that you will come across again and again. This is why correspondences are used – to focus on the appropriate type of energy you want to work with so it is exactly right and in tune with your intent. Let us consider the Elemental times in more detail.

Air

Spring is the beginning of the year, when life is starting to emerge again, and in the same way, dawn is the beginning of the day, the liminal time of transition between night and day, dark and light. For this reason Air times are good for beginnings, for new things, and may be combined very well with the New Moon as a time of beginnings.

Fire

Summer is the most active part of the year, when nature is in full bloom and life is all around us in its vigorous and active glory! Midday, when the Sun is often giving us more light and marking the most active part of the day, moving into the afternoon, is also fiery. This shows us that Fire times are good for making things grow and develop, for putting energy into things so they can move to fruition.

Water

Autumn is the counter-balance to Spring, marking the liminal time of the year before moving into the bleak cold of winter. Autumn is a time of surprises, where lots of water (as rain!) can appear out of nowhere, to disappear just as quickly leaving a glorious rainbow to mark its passing. Dusk is also a liminal time, when the light is fading and darkness is setting in. Dusk is often considered the most magickal time, when it is easiest to work magick in the gap between day and night. Water times are good for divination, the seeing in-between that comes with the liminal times.

Earth

Winter is the end of the year, when life prefers to be in the warm – be it us in our houses or some of the plants retreating into the earth! It is a time of repose, of looking within and enduring the sometimes harsh and bleak weather. Midnight as the time of transition into the next day is also a time of Earth, as the light will not come for many hours, and the patience and strength of Earth are emphasised as they also are in Winter. Earth times are good for focusing on inner change, and making plans – planting those seeds you want to grow when the weather improves and the more lively elements are dominant.

Exercise 5.3 - Elemental Times

Is there a particular time of day and time of year that you function best in? What element does each of these correspond to? Are they both the same element, and what do you think this says about the elemental balance in you?

Key Points

★ The timing of rituals is an important consideration.

★ Wiccans celebrate the eight seasonal festivals known as Sabbats or collectively as the *"Wheel of the Year"* to mark the changing seasons.

★ The phase of the Moon is a prime consideration for magickal work in Wicca.

★ The classical planets are significant in magickal traditions including Wicca.

★ The elemental times can be used to help align the nature of your magickal work.

Further Suggested Reading:

★ *Practical Planetary Magick* by Sorita d'Este and David Rankine
★ *Stations of the Sun* by Prof. Ronald Hutton
★ *The Witches Bible (Eight Sabbats for Witches)* by Janet and Stewart Farrar

---

LESSON 6

SACRED SPACE

Mankind has been building homes for their Gods for many thousands of years. Evidence of this can be found throughout history, from the megalithic stone monuments found around Britain and other parts of Europe, to the magnificent temples of Greece, Rome and Egypt, the mysterious temples of Meso-America and the temples in India as well as the modern mosques and churches. Many sacred places that exist today were built on the remains of those of the earlier religions. The temple of Artemis at Ephesus, for example, was built on what many believe to have been a sanctuary of a more ancient Mother Goddess cult, possibly that of Cybele. Many Christian churches, conversely were built on the remains  of earlier Pagan temples and shrines, often incorporating into their sacred buildings parts of the earlier stone circles, holy wells and other sacred objects. This was done in an effort to integrate the local people who were unwilling to let go of the beliefs and practices of their ancestors into the newer religion of Christ.

Wiccans, unlike some of the ancient Pagan temple religions and some other contemporary spiritual traditions today, do not build buildings from wood and stone or their Gods. Instead, we create a magick circle in which we celebrate our Gods and in which we perform our magick. The idea of a magick circle in which to perform rites is not a new one either. There are examples of circles being used as far back as ancient Babylonia, Assyria and Egypt! The practice survived through the magickians of each generation. It was used by adepts of different traditions, such as the Arab magickians of the Dark

Ages, and continued to survive through into the Renaissance through magickians such as Cornelius Agrippa, Peter de Abano, Trithemius, Dr Thomas Rudd and many others. The ceremonial magickians of the Middle Ages through to today were known to inscribe their circles with ancient divine names, such as the Tetragrammaton (YHVH) the name of God found most often in the Old Testament and believed to hold tremendous power. In fact it is believed that the proper pronunciation of the name (YHVH) has been lost and that if someone were to rediscover it today and pronounce it correctly it would cause the end of the world!

Other magickians working in these traditions used a variety of words of power to empower their circles, sometimes including symbols which represented words of power or which in themselves were believed to contain power. Another popular feature of these Renaissance magick circles was to inscribe a pentagram at each of the four cardinal points, a practice which is still found in modern Wicca.

But whereas the ceremonial magickians created their circles primarily as a protection against the spiritual beings they evoked and called up in their ceremonies, in Wicca the magic circle is created for protection together with a number of other purposes, which are discussed below:

- ★ Protection – It serves as a barrier to keep out any unwanted psychic energies and spiritual beings whilst you perform your ceremony. This helps to ensure clarity of purpose.
- ★ Container & Focus – It serves as a container for the energy raised for magickal work, allowing the practitioners to better focus, direct and use energy for results based magick, as well as for communion with the Gods.
- ★ *"Place Betwixt the Worlds"* – It serves as a meeting place between human and spirit, it is neither in this world, nor is it in the spirit world, instead it provides a gateway between the physical and astral realms.

★ The magick circle, as used in Wicca, is also symbolic of a number of things, in itself containing a special type of energy that is released as part of the ceremony, when it is properly created. Symbolism associated with the magick circle, in the context of Wiccan ceremony, includes:

★ The shape of the circle represents continuity and creation, fertility and equality

★ It can be seen to represent the womb of the Mother Goddess, the symbol of creation.

★ It may be seen to represent the Sun and/or the Moon.

★ It is a symbol of perfection – it has no beginning and no ending.

★ It is symbolic of the infinite, thus hinting at the spiralling nature of time, space etc.

The traditional size for the magick circle in the Wiccan tradition is 9ft in diameter and the circle is marked on the ground if possible, to show the physical boundaries thereof. The idea of a 9ft circle is something which the Wiccan tradition inherited from the grimoire magickians of the middle Ages and the Renaissance. However, as stated before, the circle is given a different purpose in Wicca. Likewise the number '9' is worth considering, it is a number associated with the Moon, which of course is also associated with the Mother Goddess. Again re-enforcing the symbolism already ascribed to the circle due to its shape, given above. It is important to keep in mind that even though a 9ft diameter circle is the traditional ideal, in practice today, most people working solitary may choose to create a smaller circle to suit their working space and circumstances, likewise a larger coven may choose to create a larger circle which is capable of containing all their members.

Exercise 6.1 - The Magick Circle

Record in your magickal diary the uses and symbolism of the magick circle, adding your thoughts on anything you feel is particularly significant.

RITUAL & CEREMONY

"Ritual has been called the technology of the sacred and just like any other technologies constantly changes to adapt to its circumstances..."

There are a variety of reasons for performing rituals, these may include:

★   Celebrations (Sabbats)
★   Rites of Passage (initiations, name-givings, handfastings, dedication)
★   Magickal Work (Results Magick, such as spells and healing)
★   Devotional Work (worship)

The way in which you prepare for each and the content of each ceremony will be different according to the purpose of the ceremony. Wiccan ceremony does however follow a more or less standard template, containing key ritual components. Though the key components may be adapted for different purposes and in different circumstances, their purpose, meaning and symbolism generally remains the same. It is important to learn and gain experience, which in turn will lead to understanding, of each of these component parts as you progress.

As you gain in practice and experience, you will be able to adapt these key component parts, but it is important to understand their purpose and symbolism first. It is also essential that you fully comprehend the symbolism of the work you do, the reasons for using particular tools, colours, numbers and words. Without a proper understanding of these first, you run the risk of changing the meaning of part of a ritual to such an extent that it no longer holds the same purpose and that it might also not have the desired effects as a result. This is a trap that many who are new to magickal ritual fall into (regardless of tradition), partially due to the fact that many authors encourage students to *"do what feels right"* without a full explanation. Whilst we fully agree that you should never do anything that doesn't feel right to you, you should first experiment with a variety of techniques and follow prescribed ways of working, before embarking on writing your own.

Doing this, will hopefully help you to develop a feeling, as well as an understanding, for what things are meant to feel like, before adapting them for your own use. (I.e. doing what feels right!) By doing it this way, you will be better able to fine tune different techniques for your own personal use, without running the risk of spending years reinventing the entire system, when in reality you could have used the same time and energy to progress towards more advanced practices and towards a deeper understanding of the mysteries and the Gods.

Keep in mind that many of the techniques and rituals you will read about in books or on websites, about the Wiccan tradition were written with a coven structure in mind and if you are working by yourself they may well not be suitable for use, or you will need to adapt them for use. If you need to adapt any part of a ritual for your own personal use, remember to carefully consider the words, the actions and the symbolism and spend some time thinking about whether or not it is relevant for you to include everything. There are likewise many books written for the commercial market which may contain rituals referred to as 'Wiccan' but which may in fact only be 'Wiccan inspired' – whereas of course this is still valid, it is better to study a tradition as near to its roots as possible in order to gain a competent and confident understanding of its practices. When working solitary, without the support and guidance of an experienced teacher and without the framework of a coven, this becomes even more important, as there is so much contradicting published material.

RITUAL STRUCTURE

Wiccan ceremonies usually follows a (more or less) set format, with each stage serving a particular purpose, the order a ceremony usually follows will be:

Preparation & Purification

As part of the creation of the magic circle as a sacred space in which to perform ceremonies the space is first prepared, cleansed and purified. In an ideal world we would all have a spare room set aside for the purpose of our ceremonies, but in reality this is rarely the case, so most of us have to make do with using a space which is ordinarily used for other purposes – for example a bedroom or living room. Likewise very few of us have access to private land on which to perform ceremonies, so outdoor ceremonies will also require the space to be prepared in advance for the ceremony.

To help separate ourselves from the mundane associations such a space may have it is necessary to tidy it, pack away or cover, with sheets or throws, items which might otherwise be distracting or act as triggers to remind us of the mundane world (example: turn off telephones, televisions, computers etc). It is also necessary to tidy the space as best as possible, vacuum and prepare the space to be a suitable space for you to invite the divine into. When working outdoors, it might be necessary to clear the space in daylight from any debris, litter or other obstacles – this is especially important if your ceremony will be performed in the dark, as it could prevent injuries! Also it helps you develop more of a connection to the land where you are working if you care for it by keeping it tidy.

Personal purification may also form part of the preparation work, and may take the form of a ritual bath/shower or simply washing your hands. Some groups may prepare anointing oils for use as a symbolic *'purification'* when entering the working space, a practice which also works really well for those working alone.

Purification of the ritual space

Once prepared in the physical realms, the circle space will also be purified as part of the ceremony. This is done to ensure that the energy in the space is made neutral from any unwanted energies which might be present. In some traditionally minded covens this process might be started by the sweeping of the ritual space, using the besom (broom). This is sometimes accompanied by a rhyme describing the intent of the action, an example of a popular rhyme[9] used for this purpose follow:

> *Besom, besom long and lithe*
> *Made from ash and willow withe*
> *Tied with thongs of willow bark*
> *In running stream at moonset dark.*
> *With a pentagram indighted*
> *As the ritual fire is lighted;*
> *Sweep ye circle, deosil,*
> *Sweep out evil, sweep out ill,*
> *Make the round of the ground*
> *Where we do the Lady's will.*
>
> *Besom, besom, Lady's broom*
> *Sweep out darkness, sweep out doom*
> *Rid ye Lady's hallowed ground*
> *Of demons, imps and Hell's red hound;*
> *Then set ye down on Her green earth*
> *By running stream or Mistress' hearth,*
> *'Till called once more on Sabbath night*
> *To cleans once more the dancing site*

Blessing the Salt & Water

In Wicca it is also usual to purify and consecrate the ritual space with salt and water as part of the creation of the circle. In a coven this is usually done by the High Priestess and High Priest, with the High Priestess blessing and purifying the water and the High Priest the salt. The High Priest then adds some of the consecrated salt into the water

---

[9] Attributed to Doreen Valiente

and blesses it. This is then sprinkled around the perimeter of the circle, as well as the space itself, the altar and if the participants are in the circle, they too are sprinkled. Again this is easily adapted for solitary use when the practitioner will perform both the salt and water consecrations by themselves.

Casting the magick circle

Traditionally the circle will be cast by the High Priestess (HPS) of a coven, starting at the altar in the North and walking a full circuit deosil back to the altar. The circle is cast *'deosil'* or *'sunwise'* imitating the direction and movement of the Sun through the sky. This movement is associated with the build up of energy and power and is as such perfect for creating the circle. Deosil movement in the Northern hemisphere is *'clockwise'* whilst in the Southern Hemisphere it will be *'anti-clockwise'*.

The HPS holds a sword in her outstretched hand, visualising the circle being cast from the tip of the sword as she speaks words of intent. The circle may also be cast by the High Priest, and in some instances the High Priestess or High Priest of a coven may direct another suitably experienced member of the coven to perform this task for them.

The creation of the circle is a key part of Wiccan ceremonies, it is as such also one of the most important skills someone wishing to perform ceremonies by themselves will need to learn and practice. Whereas a member of a coven will have the benefit of learning the skills necessary through group experience, solitaries will need to learn through practice and perfect their technique over a period of time through solitary experience. The circle can be erected at anytime and in any suitable space.

To begin with it will be natural to focus on the outer forms of the ritual, that is the words and the movement. But it is very important to also at all times (not just with circle casting) keep in mind that ceremony is more than just the words and actions, although those will probably be the first you will need to master, you will also need to learn to put force and energy behind your actions in order for them to have meaning and purpose.

Once the outer forms have been mastered, once you know the words and movements, you will need to also focus yourself on the inner processes which accompany them. For this it is important to train your mind through meditation and visualisation, some of the exercises provided throughout the previous lessons in this course will help you do that. Don't be discouraged if you struggle at first, it is not uncommon for it to take a great deal of practice and repetition to perfect! The important thing is to persevere! It is natural for your mind to rebel against your efforts to train it in these skills, but remember form without force is meaningless.

There are two ways in which the circle is cast when it is done by the High Priestess for her coven:

★   The circle may be cast with all the members already inside the circle space. In this the High Priestess will cast the circle around the members of the coven.

★   The circle may be cast by the High Priestess, sometimes with the help of her High Priest or another appointed person, whilst the other members of the coven wait outside the circle space. Once the circle has been cast and consecrated the other members of the coven are then brought into the circle through a gateway which is created in the North- East of the circle, typically the High Priestess' sword or the coven's besom is laid across the entrance way and each member of the coven in turn will cross it.

Each coven may have their own preferred way of creating the circle, they may even use both techniques at different times to suit the circumstances. If you are working solitary, you will obviously already be in the circle as you cast it.

Invocation of the Elemental Guardians
(The Lords of the Watchtowers)

This is done at the cardinal points of the circle, starting in the East, then in the South, West and North, using words of invocation and sometimes the elemental pentagrams. This is done using an athame, wand or fingers. Visualisation again plays an important part.

Invocation of the God and Goddess

This is done by speaking words of intent, combined with visualisation. In the context of a Coven this will take the form of *'Drawing Down the Moon'* or *'Drawing Down the Sun'* both of which requires at least two people to perform. Solitaries will usually invoke the Goddess and God into their circle, asking for their blessings on proceedings.

Magickal workings

This might be devotion, divination, healing, spells or whatever other purpose the ceremony may have. This may take many different forms and is something you need to decide by yourself (if you are working solitary) or with the other people involved (if you are part of a group or coven) on prior to performing a ceremony.

Cakes & Wine

In Wicca this is a symbolic union of the Goddess and God, by using a wand or athame (representing the masculine divine) and the chalice (representing the feminine divine) and combining them. In a coven this part of the ceremony will be performed by the High Priestess and High Priest, but it could also be done by just one person in a solitary rite. The alternative to this, if you working by yourself, is to simply ask for the blessing of the Gods on the food and drink you have prepared in the ceremony and consuming it as part of ritual grounding.

Following Cakes & Wine, the ceremony is concluded. This is done by thanking and bidding farewell to The God, Goddess (and any other spiritual beings invoked during the ceremony), thanking and banishing the Elemental Guardians and a ritual deconstruction of the magick circle.

We will now consider each of these steps in turn:

Blessing Salt & Water

You will need:

* ★ 2 small bowls, one with salt (preferably sea salt), the other with water (preferably spring water).
* ★ Optional: Athame or Wand
* ★ Pentacle

The salt and water should be placed into the two bowls respectively and placed, alongside the other tools on the altar. The use of water and salt, representing the feminine elements of water and earth, emphasises the symbolism of the circle as representing the Goddess, and also demonstrates the union of the physical (symbolised by salt) and the astral (symbolised by water), implying the function of the circle as gateway between the realms.

The bowl of water is placed on the pentacle and the tip of the athame, wand or finger placed in the water. As this is done words are spoken whilst gold light is visualised passing from your heart down your arm through the hand (or athame). Whilst doing this say:

"I bless and consecrate this water, symbol of the tides of life and death, that it be pure and untainted, in the names of the Goddess and the God."

The same procedure is followed for the salt, saying:

"I bless and consecrate this salt, symbol of purity and protection, in the names of the Goddess and God."

Some of the salt is then poured into the water and stirred, the consecrated salt water is then sprinkled around the perimeter of the Circle, onto the altar, and into the centre of the circle. You can also anoint yourself with some of the water by touching it to your third eye.

Casting the Circle

<u>You will need:</u>

★   *Optional:* Athame or Wand

When you work solitary the best tools for casting the circle are the athame or wand, or alternatively you can use your hand. The sword is not really very practical for solitary work, but if you have one as well as sufficient space in which to work you could of course use it. The circle is usually cast starting from the North (as the place of Earth), or sometimes the East (as the place of beginnings). Wherever the starting point, a full clockwise (deosil) circuit is delineated so the circle caster ends up back at the place that she started.

The circle is cast with the sword or athame, or if outdoors often with a wand. It can equally be cast with the hand, using the index finger of your preferred hand. The standard circle size is nine foot in diameter, which could be marked or visualised. As the circle is cast, the caster and anyone else present should visualise blue flames forming at the boundary of the circle, from the tip of the casting tool, be it sword, athame wand or hand. Whilst doing so you should say:

"By the Air that is Her breath, by the Fire of Her bright spirit, by the ever-living Waters of Her womb and by the Earth that is Her body, the circle is cast, so mote it be."

Again alternative words may be used to state the intent of the circle casting. To remove the circle at the end of the ceremony, the HPS always starts in the north, and moves in the direction opposite to the Sun (widdershins, which is anticlockwise in the Northern Hemisphere) back to the north, with everyone seeing the blue flames dying away as she moves around the circle, speaking words like those for casting, except changing the end to say, *"the circle is open"* rather than *"the circle is cast"*. If you use the words given for the casting procedure above, you would also reverse the order in which the elements are named, as you will be going through the quarters of the circle in a different order, therefore:

"By the Earth that is Her body by the ever-lasting Waters of Her womb, by the Fire of Her bright Spirit and by the Air that is Her breath, the circle is open, yet unbroken."

Invoking the Elemental Guardians

You will need:
★   Optional: Athame or Wand

The Elemental Guardians are always called (invoked) in the same sequence, beginning in the East with Air, and moving clockwise around the circle, ending with Earth in the North. Movement within a circle is always done in a clockwise manner, unless you are banishing or bidding farewell. The calling of the Elemental Guardians has three components which are all combined together. These are the words, the gestures and the visualisation. The words declare your intent to the Elemental Guardians and to the universe, the gestures demonstrate respect for the Guardians you are calling, and the visualisation helps define the form the Guardians manifest into or through.

When an element is called you begin by raising your arms in the blessing position. This is done by raising your arms so they form a "V", with your palms open and facing forwards. You then would perform the call, the following invocations are good for simple solitary rituals, you can adapt them as you gain in experience to suit your own preferences:

★   East/Air
"I face to the East, sacred place of Air. Guardians of the Element of Air, I call to you and ask you to join me here in my rite; share your qualities of joy, clarity and memory with me and guard my circle. I bid you Hail and Welcome."

★   South/Fire
"I face to the South, sacred place of Fire. Guardians of the Element of Fire, I call to you and ask you to join me here in my rite; share your qualities of

creativity, willpower and passion with me and guard my circle. I bid you Hail and Welcome."

★   West/Water
"I face to the West, sacred place of Water. Guardians of the Element of Water, I call to you and ask you to join me here in my rite; share your qualities of healing, intuition and emotion with me and guard my circle. I bid you Hail and Welcome."

★   North/Earth
"I face to the North, sacred place of Earth. Guardians of the Element of Earth, I call to you and ask you to join me here in my rite; share your qualities of steadfastness, perseverance and strength with me and guard my circle. I bid you Hail and Welcome."

It is usual for a small bow to be given towards each direction following the invocation as a sign of respect to the Guardian. The same is done when they are banished at the end of the rite. Whether working solitary or in a coven it is usual for everyone to face the direction in which the Guardian is being invoked. For the farewells they are performed in reverse to the calls, starting in the North and working anticlockwise ending in the East.

★   East/Air
"Again I face to the East, sacred place of Air. Guardians of the Element of Air, I thank you for your presence in my circle here tonight. For now I bid you Hail & Farewell!"

★   South/Fire
"Again I face to the South, sacred place of Fire. Guardians of the Element of Fire, I thank you for your presence in my circle here tonight. For now I bid you Hail & Farewell!"

★   West/Water
"I face to the West, sacred place of Water. Guardians of the Element of Water, I thank you for your presence in my circle here tonight. For now I bid you Hail & Farewell!"

★ North/Earth

"I face to the North, sacred place of Earth. Guardians of the Element of Earth, I thank you for your presence in my circle here tonight. For now I bid you Hail & Farewell!"

Exercise 6.2 – Circle Casting

Write up the blessing of salt & water, circle casting and calling of the guardians of the watchtowers in your magickal diary, leaving space for any notes you may wish to add. Practice the blessing of salt and water, circle casting and calling the guardians until you are comfortable with it.

Record in your magickal diary how this makes you feel, and any changes you notice as you practice.

Invoking the Goddess & God

When performing invocations it is common to face the altar, which is in the North, a place associated with the Gods and with Mystery. Some people memorise invocations they have prepared beforehand, and others prefer free-form invocations. In either case it is always worthwhile to have spent some time researching the deities in question, learning about their qualities and myths so aspects of these can be included in the invocations. Roles and titles, symbols and sacred animals are all often included in invocations. Invocations are a key part of the devotional aspect of Wicca, as they are a declaration of your intent to bring the energy of the Divine Feminine and Masculine into your ceremonies, and also of your reverence for those divine forces.

In a similar way to the Elemental Guardians, when bidding farewell to the Goddess and God, the same or similar words are usually used, removing any words that are not appropriate, and ending with *"Hail and Farewell"*. Following this you will find examples of an invocation to the Horned God, who in the Wiccan Tradition is sometimes named as the Celtic God Cernunnos, as depicted on the Gundestrup Cauldron; and an invocation to the

Goddess, who is sometimes invoked as Diana, the Roman Goddess associated with the Moon and with the wild animals of the Earth. You can use these invocations as is, adapt them or alternatively have a go at writing your own!

Invocation of the God

Mighty Horned Lord
Lord of Light and Lord of Dark
Lord of the Wild Beasts and the Wild Places
Guardian, hunter and teacher
Lord of the Dance of Life and Death
I call to you and ask you to join me here
Bring your magick, your inspiration, your freedom and your strength
Fill me with your timeless wisdom and wonder
You who are the quickening vigour of the sap
And the rutting stag
You who are the mighty oak and the thunder in the heavens
Mighty Horned Lord
Wild and free, wise and mighty
Be present in my rite and bless me with your power
I bid you hail and welcome

Invocation of the Goddess

Beautiful Lady of Life
You who are the radiant Moon in the sky
And the fertile Earth beneath my feet
Creatrix, sustainer and inspirer
Mistress of magick and dreams
Queen of the heavens and of nature
Nurturing mother and fierce warrior
I ask you to bless me in my rite
Infuse me with your love and your magick
Inspire and guide me as I honour you and your ways
Fill me with your beauty and strength
Be present in my rite and bless me with your wisdom
I bid you hail and welcome

Cakes & Wine

You will need:

* ★ Wine, Mead, Ale or Fruit Juice
* ★ Bread, Cake or Biscuits
* ★ A Chalice (Cup or Wine Glass will suffice)
* ★ A Pentacle (You can make your own using a disk of wood, metal or wax and inscribing a pentagram on it)
* ★ A small plate or other suitable container on which to place the bread or cakes.

The ceremony of the Blessing of the Cakes & Wine takes place after most of the work and celebration are done in the circle. The blessing of the wine in sometimes called the *"Symbolic Great Rite"* as it symbolises the union of Goddess & God, which is considered to be one of the key mysteries of Wicca, and which can only be fully understood through direct experience.

The emphasis is on polarity, with the Chalice symbolising the reproductive organs of the Goddess and the athame the phallus of the Horned God, the fertilizing principle. In a coven it is usual for the High Priestess and High Priest to perform the ceremony together, the High Priest holding the Chalice, and the High Priestess lowering the athame into the Chalice saying:

"As the Athame is to the Male so the Cup is to the Female and conjoined they bring forth fruitfulness."

The Cakes are often said to form part of the grounding of the ritual and also symbolise the fruitfulness of the Goddess and God, as well as symbolising the gifts given to us by the Earth Herself. However their symbolic use is as a sacrament, for they are consumed after being blessed with the divine energy. When working in a group it is traditional to have one more cake than the number of celebrants for the blessing. The last cake is used to make a libation to the Goddess & God or the Spirits of the place.

When working solitary you can perform the ceremony as follows. Hold the athame in your dominant hand (or use your hand, with the forefinger extended in place of the athame), and place the chalice on the pentacle. Lower the athame into the chalice and as you do so imagine the energy of the God descending down the blade of the athame (or your hand) into the wine, like a flash of golden lightning, and the energy of the Goddess permeating the wine, like a flowing tide, from the chalice that symbolises her reproductive organs. Take the Chalice and hold it up saying:

"Great Goddess bless this wine as a symbol of your fruitfulness and love. May I never thirst!"

Take a sip of the wine and replace the Chalice on the altar.

Now place the cake on the plate on the pentacle, hold your hands over it and visualise golden energy flowing through your hands down into the cake as you say:

"Lord and Lady I ask that you bless these cakes a symbol of your union and love. May I never hunger!"

Break the cake in half and eat half – replacing the remaining part on the plate on the pentacle or offer it to the nature spirits if you are working outdoors.

Exercise 6.3 – Blessing the Cakes & Wine

Record the blessing of the Cakes & Wine in your magickal diary, and practice the ceremony until you are comfortable with it.
You may try and adapt the words, using your own whilst keeping the symbolism and purpose of the ceremony in mind.

THE ALTAR

Like the ancient traditions of our ancestors, Wiccans also create an altar on which representations of the Goddess and God they are working with, together with the working tools for the ceremony are placed. Typically this is placed in the North of the Circle, or in some traditions it may be placed in the East or in the centre. When you first start doing ceremonies, it may be a good idea to have the altar in the East as this is symbolically the place of new beginnings.

When you are working indoors it is a good idea to have a box, cabinet or small table for use as your altar. Outdoors you may do the same or you may prefer to take a cloth and spread it on the ground, placing the items appropriately on it. The altar is a functional working space, so as you will see it is arranged for practical convenience as well as symbolism.

Normally tools are placed according to their elemental correspondences. Thus you would normally have the pentacle (Earth) in the north, the wand and censer (Air) in the east, the Athame (Fire) in the south and the chalice (Water) in the west. However you need to be practical, so be sure to place items that you will need in easily accessibly places. For example the salt and water bowls should be near the front of the altar, and any spell ingredients should be easy to reach. The candles representing the Goddess and God should be placed at the back of the altar, with the black candle for the Goddess on the left as you look at the altar, and the white candle for the God on the right. A candle to represent Spirit is then placed in the middle between them. You can also add statues and other items to decorate the altar, particularly if it is a seasonal celebration, but remember that ultimately your altar is a practical working space.

Exercise 6.4 - Your Altar

Record in your magickal diary the basic altar set-up you use for ceremonies. You may find it helpful to draw this as a simple birds-eye view from above.

Tools

We have already looked at the tools used in Wiccan ceremonies. Ideally you should make the tools you need yourself, or purchase them from a reputable craftsperson. Many ordinary household objects can also be used, but remember to consecrate them first. For example a wine glass or old goblet can be used as a chalice, a small round cutting board can be made into a pentacle, a wand can be carved from a piece of fallen wood (preferably the wood of a fruit or nut bearing tree), an ordinary knife can be used as an athame. Do however remember that any objects you use as ritual tools should be kept for that purpose only once they are consecrated, this will help retain the power raised through your rituals and make the tools more potent with time.

If you are going to purchase a tool, and if at all possible, you should try and see and touch the tools you purchase before you commit yourself to it. So if there are festivals or conferences, with a marketplace, taking place near to where you live, it is worth attending and browsing through, comparing the different tools. Though it is tempting to purchase elaborate tools, simple is often best, and most importantly you should choose something which you are comfortable with.

Key Points

★ Wiccans create a magick circle as their sacred space.

★ The magick circle serves as a protection, a container for the energy raised, and a place *'between the worlds.'*

★ The casting of the magick circle has several components, which serve to establish the space as an effective magickal temple.

★ The blessing of Cakes & Wine in Wiccan ceremonies acts as a Eucharistic sacrament.

★ The altar is a practical working space set up with symbolic significance.

Further Optional Reading:

★ *Circle of Fire* by Sorita d'Este & David Rankine
★ *Horns of Power: Manifestations of the Horned God* edited by Sorita d'Este (various contributors)
★ *Lid of the Cauldron* by Patricia Crowther
★ *The Wiccan Mystic* by Ben Gruagach
★ *Wicca* by Viviane Crowley
★ *Witchcraft for Tomorrow* by Doreen Valiente
★ *The Witches Bible* by Janet Farrar & Stewart Farrar

Lesson 7

Initiation & Rites Of Passage

Rites of passage are as old as mankind. In the past, as they do today, rites of passage marked important stages in life. Ceremonies to mark rites of passage are still performed throughout the world – even in modern Western Society – we have ceremonies to mark birth (baptism, name-givings), adulthood (18th or 21st birthdays), marriage and death (funerals). Some cultures also still celebrate menarche (first menstruation). Likewise we still find *'initiation'* ceremonies in many cultural and economic situations – some formal, some simple acts like being shown around and introduced to new work colleagues or inductions at college or university.

Initiation ceremonies are a key part of the Wiccan Tradition. It is through initiation that one becomes a member of a tradition, and indeed a member of a coven. In traditional covens, such as those of the Alexandrian or Gardnerian traditions, initiation is the only way through which someone may learn about the inner mysteries of the tradition. Today there are many who continue to work in such groups, which are often very private, whilst some choose to learn and practice through learning from books and sometimes creating their own traditions with friends who share their interests.

A distinction needs to be made between those who work in the esoteric (initiated) traditions and those who work in the exoteric (non-initiate) ways. In the same way, for example, in the mystery cults of ancient Greece, the distinction was made between those who were initiates and the uninitiated, or magickal practitioners and non-practitioners.

Initiation into the tradition, or indeed initiation into any initiatory tradition, is what distinguishes it from a purely social or celebratory organisation or group. Initiation marks the opening of a veil into the mysteries of life and death, whereby the initiate undertakes a journey which all other members of the coven also undertook themselves. It marks a point of beginning for the newly initiated member from whereon they are able to work with, experience and share in the inner mysteries of the coven and of the tradition. In this lesson we will consider the differences, together with the benefits of working in both the esoteric and exoteric traditions, as well as the meanings behind the different degrees (and titles) found in Wicca.

WICCAN INITIATIONS

As already stated, initiation rites are usually practiced by those working within covens of the esoteric traditions of Wicca, such as in the Alexandrian or Gardnerian Traditions – but also in many other traditions which have developed out of these over the years. During the First Degree initiation the postulant (candidate or probationer) is welcomed into the both the coven and tradition in a formal ceremony. The ceremony is one which all initiates undertake and as such it becomes a shared experience between the members of the coven. During the ceremony the new initiate also makes their own personal commitment towards both the tradition and the coven, in addition to their commitment to the Goddess and God.

There are three main initiations in the Wiccan Tradition, the titles given at each initiation may vary according to the tradition, but usually these are:

★ First Degree – Initiation as a Witch & Priest(ess) – or just as a Witch
★ Second Degree – Elevation to the role of a Priest(ess) or as a High Priest(ess)
★ Third Degree – Elevation to the role of an independent High Priestess or High Priest

Some covens also have a fourth rite of passage as part of their membership procedures, which is called 'Dedication' and is performed at the start of an individual's journey with the group – in other words before undertaking the First Degree Initiation. The ways in which the degrees are given may vary greatly from coven to coven and from tradition to tradition, as such it is not unusual for someone to undergo these stages more than once, if they move between different groups. Initiation ceremonies may symbolise different things or mark different rites of passage depending on the tradition, likewise the titles and meanings of the degrees may also vary between groups and are usually not considered to be valued outside of the group structure, other than in a very generic manner.

So for instance, a Wiccan High Priestess of 3rd degree, would usually only use the title of High Priestess, within the context of the work she is doing within the tradition or group she works in – rather than using it as a title when she is dining out with friends or chatting on an internet forum, unless it within the context of the conversation of course. Initiation requires the commitment and the involvement of the candidate undertaking it. It is always undertaken of *'free will and accord'* and as such the candidate partakes in the journey, because they want to and because they have been given the opportunity to do so with a group of people they feel comfortable with and want to learn with. Initiation might be a shared experience as previously stated, but the journey undertaken and experienced by each individual will of course always be unique.

Coven Dedication (Probationer) – Commitment

As mentioned above, many covens today also have a fourth ceremony which may be considered an *'initiation'*, as it does mark a new beginning. This is the Dedication Ceremony, which is sometimes called probationer or neophyte dedication or acceptance rite. This is the ceremony in which a potential member of a coven is officially taken on as a trainee and the point at which their probationer period starts and as such they become a candidate for initiation into the coven. This should not be confused with initiation into a coven or for that matter initiation into the tradition of Wicca – that can only be achieved through the ceremony of First Degree initiation. Dedication fulfils a different role all together – providing both the individual and the coven with a period of time to get to know each other better, whilst the Probationer is given the opportunity to show that they are able to commit the time, energy and will be able to work as part of the team if they should indeed progress to initiation.

In our own groups, this ceremony is focused on the would be member committing themselves to the study of the tradition with the group they are joining, before the members of the group, as well as the coven Gods and the Guardians of the Elements.

Remember:

★ Dedication to a coven does not make you a Wiccan Initiate
★ Dedication precedes First Degree Initiation
★ Dedication is not practiced by all covens.
★ Dedication is also sometimes called neophyte or probationer dedication or acceptance rite.

First Degree Initiation – Rite of Rebirth

Those who seek initiation into a coven and who find a group which suits their needs and which is able to offer them a place, will first encounter a period of evaluation, as well as in some instances, a period of training. For some traditions this period lasts for a *'year and a day'* (i.e. thirteen full moons) after which the candidate may request initiation from their High Priestess or High Priest. If accepted, they will undergo a ceremony which is a symbolic death and rebirth, through which they become a member of the tradition. This is the first degree initiation, in which they are given the title of *'Witch'* or *'Witch & Priest/ess'* and in which they take (or in some instances, are given) a new magickal or witch name. This name is only used within the context of coven meetings and is never shared with anyone who is not also an initiate of the tradition.

The purpose of First Degree initiation is to align the new member with the magickal current of the tradition and with that of the coven – it marks a new beginning, both as a member of the tradition and of the group. As such it can also be thought of as a rebirth or welcoming into the group/tradition after which they will be taught about the inner mysteries of the coven and will be taught the ceremonies, expected to copy the Book of Shadows by hand, and more about the inner workings of the tradition. Many describe the experience as a *'coming home'* in which they join a *'Family'* of their choosing, who share their beliefs and practices.

The symbol which is most often associated with this degree is the water triangle – i.e. an equilateral triangle pointing downwards. This symbol is also symbolic of the Wiccan Goddess.

Second Degree Initiation – Personal Power

Second Degree initiation (or elevation) marks a point at which the initiate has learned all the techniques necessary to lead others in ritual. When an initiate has both sufficient knowledge and experience to do so, s/he may approach their High Priest or High Priestess and asked to be given Second Degree. Covens and traditions vary in their requirements for this degree, but it is usual for someone to be an initiate of the First Degree for at least a year-and-a-day before they would be considered for Second Degree, though in most instances it takes much longer – firstly because not everyone may have a desire to undertake this elevation, unless they also wish to take on more responsibility and secondly because it takes a great deal of study, work and commitment to undertake this elevation which is a mark of personal achievement.

Furthermore, Second Degree marks a *'coming into your own power'* for the initiate and usually a person will need to be able to demonstrate this both in their Craft practices and their mundane life. During this elevation ceremony the initiate is given the title of *'Priest/ess'* or *'High Priest/ess'* (depending on the tradition) and they can, if they wish (or circumstances dictate) leave their own coven to hive and form their own *Daughter Coven*. This process is called *'hiving'* and a person undertaking this will need at least two other people to join them in the new coven – these may also be members of their *'mother coven'* who wish to join the new coven or might be people who they themselves have trained and who are ready to be initiated as members of the new Coven. A second degree initiate running their own coven would usually do so under the supervision of their *'Mother Coven'* (i.e. the one they worked with first, and into which they were initiated) until they have undertaken third degree. The symbol of the second degree is an upside down (i.e. two points up) pentagram, which symbolises the Horned God.

Third Degree - Sacred Marriage & Independence

Third Degree initiation within the Wiccan tradition marks the point at which an initiate becomes fully independent from their initiators. As such, they will need to be able to take full responsibility for the running of their own coven on all levels.

Requirements for this degree vary between traditions, but it is usually only given to someone who has demonstrated their ability in running a coven for a period of time with success – that is showing that they are able to take responsibility in regards to leading, initiating and teachings others in the tradition.

Additionally they will need to demonstrate their own ability to transcend their own ego through being able to channel the Gods fully so that they will be able to take part in the *Great Rite* (The Sacred Marriage) which is a symbolic union of the Goddess and God in the Wiccan tradition. This sometimes misunderstood ceremony can be performed as a sexual (actuality) or non-sexual (symbolic) rite. The Great Rite is usually only done in actuality if those concerned are already in an established love relationship and is only ever done in this way if both parties agree.

The symbol of the Third Degree is the pentagram topped with a triangle. The pentagram is one point up, and likewise the triangle points upwards. This symbol symbolises the union of the Goddess and the God, as the upward pointing pentagram symbolises the Goddess and a triangle with one point upwards is a symbol of Fire, which symbolises the God.

Exercise 7.1 - The Three Degrees

Write down the key points regarding the three degrees, including their symbols, in your magickal diary.

Key Points

★ Rites of passage mark life changes, both in the exoteric and esoteric world.

★ Initiation marks the beginning of a spiritual journey of self-transformation.

★ Some covens practice a dedication ceremony prior to initiation as part of the process of ensuring compatibility and dedication.

★ There are three degrees of initiation in the Wiccan tradition.

★ The First Degree initiation is a symbolic death and rebirth which marks the alignment of the new initiate to their coven.

★ The Second Degree initiation marks a coming into power, and at this point an initiate can hive to form their own coven if they choose.

★ The Third Degree initiation marks the full independence of an initiate, who can run a fully autonomous coven.

Self-Dedication – Solitary Commitment

It is not always possible for those interested in practising Wicca to find a suitable coven in their area, for some it is simply not possible to commit the time and energy that being a member of a coven requires. For this reason many people decide to work and learn by themselves, working from published material and sometimes supplementing their learning by attending public workshops and lectures on related subjects where these are available. Self-dedication is a solitary pursuit, which is between the practitioner and their Gods, whereas initiation into a coven is done in the presence of the Gods and peers.

The purpose of initiation into the Wiccan tradition is manifold, but one of the key purposes is that it marks the welcoming of a person into a coven and into a tradition.

It is not possible for a person working alone to welcome themselves into either a tradition or into a coven, as there will be neither a tradition nor a Coven involved in the process. However, this puts those working alone in a difficult position should they wish to make a more permanent commitment. The solution to this is to perform a Self-dedication ceremony, in which they dedicate themselves towards the study and practice of the tradition, in the presence of the Gods and elemental guardians. This practice is something which has developed out of a need during the last few decades and although it does not form a *'traditional'* part of Wicca, it is one which is widely practiced today.

This form of dedication is not the same as any of the traditional degrees found in the esoteric traditions; nor should it be confused with that of a dedication done when joining a coven. This is something quite different and, as the name indicates, it is a personal experience and is one that is usually done after a period of study and reflection, rather than at the start of it, as the case is with a coven dedication. Self-dedication to the path of Wicca will usually involve the individual making a promise to themselves, and vows to their deities to commit themselves to the path of continuing their studies and practices of Wicca. As a result, many who undertake such a ceremony do, when their circumstances change, seek initiation into a coven in order to further their studies and experience of the tradition.

Self-dedication should be taken very seriously, it is not something to lightly step into thinking *"...oh, that's a nice idea..."* A person undertaking self-dedication does so of their own free will and they should make very sure that it is something they really want to undertake – or indeed need to undertake. They don't have the benefit of the experience of a High Priestess or High Priest who can guide them through the process, which those who join a Coven has, nor do they have the group support which comes with being part of (or a trainee to) a Coven. The responsibility for everything falls firmly on the shoulders of the person undertaking it.

Furthermore, whereas a person undertaking dedication to a Coven will be undergoing a ceremony facilitated by others (the High Priestess, High Priest and other members of the Coven), those undertaking a self-Dedication have to facilitate the ceremony for themselves. For this reason it is a good idea to spend at least a year exploring, studying and learning about the ceremonies, beliefs and symbolism of the Wiccan tradition – before embarking on a self-dedication. You will after all need to be able to write the ceremony yourself, as well as conduct it yourself – so you will need to be comfortable and confident to cast and purify your own Circle, invoke the Guardians of the four quarters yourself, as well as of course the deities of your choice. You will also need to construct your own vows and promises to make during the ceremony – this is not an easy task even for people with a few years experience of working with others, so it's a mammoth (if not impossible) task for someone who has just read their first book, no matter how good that book is!

A further reason for a period of study and gaining solitary experience is to ensure that you are making the right decision – one might be all excited about it when you first start out, but it takes time to explore the ins and outs and to decide whether it is something you truly wish to dedicate your life to! That is a pretty big decision, think of it like marriage – unless you are a very impulsive person, you are unlikely to marry just anyone you meet after a few days, just because it seems like a good idea doesn't make it so. It might work out – but it also might not, so spare yourself the trouble and take your time! Self-Dedication might not replace a Coven Initiation (or Dedication) but it is no less serious – it fulfils a different role, but one which nonetheless will have a lasting impact on the lives of those who do it.

Exercise 7.2 - Self Dedication v. Coven Dedication

Compare self-dedication and coven dedication, making a list of the pros and cons of both. Does either appeal to you, and if so why?

Key Points:

★ There is no *'traditional'* self-dedication rite. Each ceremony is unique to the person performing it

★ Self-dedication does not replace, nor is it the same as any of the traditional Wiccan Initiations

★ A period of study preceding a self-dedication is highly recommended!

OTHER INITIATIONS

As you would (or at least should!) have already noticed, the magickal world is full of confusing terminology – especially when you are first starting out. The same words are sometimes used to mean different things in different systems and traditions. Many of the Pagan and magickal traditions, other than Wicca, also use the term *'Initiation'* and some have other words for ceremonies marking an initiatory experience.

In some instances undergoing an initiation is still the only form of progression in a tradition, this is true for example of the Hermetic Order of the Golden Dawn and Ordo Templi Orientis in which there are several levels of initiation, each corresponding to one of the Spheres on the Tree of Life (Qabalah). The practitioner undertakes an initiation only after a period of careful study and practice – on which they will are tested before they may progress. In some modern Golden Dawn traditions the use of *'self-initiation'* or *'astral initiation'* is accepted for the lower grades, though this is often a point that causes serious disputes from the more traditional orders.

In some forms of traditional witchcraft there is only one initiation, in which the person is accepted into the coven, the terminology will vary a great deal between traditions. There are no *'degrees'* and the High Priest and High Priestess are the elders of the tradition and in many instances, the roles can only be held by a hand-fasted or married couple.

In the *Fellowship of Isis* those wishing to undertake a commitment are ordained (a term also used in the Church) as a priestess or a priest and dedicate themselves during this ceremony to the service of three Goddesses. After a further period of study and work an Ordained Priest or Priestess can undertake the next level and receive Ordination as a Priestess Hierophant or a Priest Hierophant, again dedicating themselves to three Goddesses.

Some who work within the Western Mystery Tradition also believe that there is only *'one true'* initiation, that is an initiation that comes from the ultimate divine and one which cannot be facilitated by another person or group of people. This initiation is a private matter between the individual concerned and their Gods, it is not one which can be requested, nor is it one which one can decide to undertake. It might be awakened or encouraged through initiation into a magickal order or tradition, through which the individual is able to gain experience and learn, but it is not equal to it. True Initiation is usually concerned with the achievement of the Great Work, which can be seen as the perfected union with the self and the Universe and it may take the form of several events throughout ones life, it may be brought on by a magickal or seemingly mundane experiences. This type of initiation is also not one which is boasted about, as the transcendence of personal ego is inherent in it. So, effectively, someone who claims to have received it is likely to be fooling themselves or trying to inflate their ego.

For Wiccans, First Degree initiation is a ceremony of rebirth, in which the person being initiated undergoes a symbolic transformation and becomes a member of the tradition. It is also their official introduction to the God and Goddess of the tradition (or Coven) and their welcoming into the Coven itself. The functions of this initiation are thus manifold, but should not be confused or conflated with that of other traditions. It is also important to keep in mind that someone may be an initiate of more than one tradition, at the same time, so it is necessary to say 'Wiccan Initiate' or '- insert name of tradition- initiate' to avoid confusion when discussing the matter outside of the Wiccan community.

OTHER RITES OF PASSAGE

Some Wiccans also practice other rites of passage. These include naming ceremonies for babies; funerary rites, Requiems; and wedding rites which are known as *'Handfastings'*.

Naming Ceremonies

Some people wish to mark the birth of a newborn baby into their family with a ceremony and as such they may perform *'name-givings'* (sometimes called *'Wiccanings'*) for the child. These ceremonies are performed by Wiccans and are also commonly used by other Pagan groups. By their very nature, the ceremonies are individual and are usually written and performed by the child's parents or a close friend. Name-giving ceremonies, unlike their Christian equivalent of Baptism, are not a way of bringing a child into the tradition or religion of the parents, but instead are a rite during which the parents ask the Gods for their blessings on the child, for protection and guidance in how to raise their child and during which other members of the family (or Coven) can make their own promises in regards to helping with the child's upbringing.

Handfastings

Handfasting is the Pagan equivalent of a wedding and is the ceremonial affirmation of the desire of a couple to be bonded together and have their love and commitment for each other formally seen by friends and family. Traditionally handfasting last for a year-and-a-day after which a couple may choose to recommit to each other again, some people however perform a handfasting to last for as *'long as love lasts'* - meaning that the vows to each other will be valid for as long as love prospers between the couple.

The idea for handfasting comes from an old Scottish custom, where a couple would have their hands tied together in a simple ceremony, and if they were still together a year later, they were accepted as man and wife. This was still practiced into the nineteenth century. In the last fifty years it has become traditional to perform handfasting at Beltane (Mayday) or the Summer Solstice, the being the times when the weather is best and nature at its most abundant and beautiful. The term tying the knot, which is still used widely today, originates with the practise of handfasting. During the ceremony the couples' hands are tied together with a red cord (red symbolises the desire, passion and vitality of the love the couple have for each other). The cord which is used is often kept by the couple as a reminder of their vows.

A red ribbon can be used instead of a cord, if this is preferred and if there is another colour that is appropriate, it can be used instead. Handfasting rituals are usually written by the couple themselves, or by the Priest/ess who will be leading the ceremony with some personal input from the couple.

Funerary Rites

Death can be considered to be the last rite of passage, in which a person's soul passes from this life to the next. Many Wiccans believe in reincarnation, in which the soul passes from this life to rest for a while in the Summerlands, a place of perfection, until it is ready to reincarnate again and continue its journey in the world. Our ancestors had many rites of passage for the dead and many different beliefs concerning death, just like we do today. It is important both for the person who has passed on and for those who stay behind to mark the occasion. For Wiccans death is not an ending, it is just another step in the spiral of life and as such it is not something that is mourned, but instead the life of the person who died is celebrated. Ceremonies marking death are as individual as those they are done for. They are usually performed by a close friend who shared the same spiritual path and in the case of Wiccans, often by a member of their Coven.

COVEN VS. SOLITARY

Although many people want to work in a coven, there are many who are not able to do so due to circumstances. For instance it may be that in your local area there are no Wiccan covens or that family or career takes up a large proportion of your time making it difficult for you to commit the time and energy to coven Life. There are also people who simply prefer to work by themselves or with one working partner. And of course even if you want to work in a coven it is not always easy to find the 'right' group for you and your own particular needs.

Working in a coven requires a great deal of time and commitment. The learning process you experience as a probationer before initiation becomes more intense after initiation when you are actually in the coven.

Working Alone

Working alone, for most people, is the best way to start - whether you end up joining a coven or decide to stay solitary. It allows you to explore your beliefs and a variety of practises so that you can find what works for you. If your ultimate goal is to join a coven, they are likely to be more favourable towards someone who has some experience and knowledge already, as this shows dedication and commitment which are important qualities coven leaders will look for. Working as a solitary allows you to be as eclectic as you wish to be, and as creative as your heart desires.

Pros and cons of working by yourself:
* It's a good way to start learning.
* You can pace your own learning speed and experience according to your own personal needs.
* You only have yourself to consider and no group pressure.
* You can do your rituals at times and on days that suit you.

★ It can get lonely without someone to share your experiences with.

★ You are on your own if you experience problems.

★ You do not have a peer group to measure your progress with and keep your earthed.

★ It is a good way to find out if the tradition you are exploring is *'for you'* without having to make any commitments.

Working In A Coven

So what is it like working in a Wiccan coven? Well, we like to think of a coven as an extended family, the family you choose for yourself and the family which chooses you. This refers to the close bonds that develop (over time, its not going to be there from the first day!) between people who do magick and devotion together. The essence of this bond is captured in the words *'perfect love and perfect trust'* (sometimes abbreviated to PLPT) which play an important role in the traditions' initiation ceremonies.

Before you even consider joining a coven - do your research! Learn as much as you can by reading books by authors from the tradition you are considering. Doing this course in itself will already have provided you with some insights – both about the way the tradition works and how you feel about some aspects of it. All this will help you on your path, but it is important to also keep an open mind, making sure that you are making the right choices along the way. Sometimes it is necessary to put traditions aside and look at groups from a different perspective –

★ Will you fit in with the existing group?

★ Will that group be able to offer you training and opportunities for the experience you seek?

★ Will you be able to make the commitments the group expects from you?

★ Do you agree with the key principles of the group – for example, their beliefs and practices?

Once you are certain, in your heart, that you would like to start practising Wicca as your spiritual path, the best way to start is by performing some ceremonies by yourself. Celebrate a few of the seasonal celebrations, mark the different phases of the Moon in your own way. Consider setting up a seasonal shrine in your home and learn as much as you can – by reading, speaking to people and experimenting with different techniques that appeal to you. Attending public events (where available) will give you a chance to meet other likeminded people, go to a variety of talks/workshops by people from different traditions and experience public group rituals. This contact with other people interested in or already practising Wicca or another tradition will help expand your knowledge and give you insights into some of the many options open to you.

Before approaching a group for membership consider how much time you can devote to a group, it sounds simple, but time can be a big obstacle for some people. Find out what the group you are considering will expect from you. For example:

★ Do they meet for the 8 seasonal Sabbats? [8 meetings a year = 8]
★ Will you need to attend Esbats (Full Moon ceremonies?) [13 meetings a year = 21]
★ Will you need to attend other meetings or workshops?

Also find out whether or not you will be expected to do work away from the group – studies or projects will all take up some of your time. There are groups which meet once a week, some which meet twice a week – and others which meet only at the occasion of the major Sabbats (i.e. four times a year!) – and of course everything in between. Take into consideration that members of a coven may be expected to turn up early for ceremonies to help set up the temple space – this may involve cleaning tools, vacuuming the room and even dusting! There are many other *'mundane'* tasks which will need doing too – allow extra time for this.

Then consider the financial implications on your life. Can you afford it? No reputable coven will expect you to pay for training or initiations, however you need to take into consideration other expenses which you may incur as part of being a member.

★ The first is travelling – if you are lucky and live near to the covenstead this might not be an issue, but many people travel long distances to attend meetings and this might be expensive, especially if meetings are frequent. Likewise, it might also add to the time commitment, so do take it into consideration.

★ Tools – although you won't need that many tools to begin with, you will be expected to have some personal tools. There are many ways of obtaining less expensive tools, making it yourself or improvising – but it is still worth bearing in mind that this might be an expense you will incur along the way.

★ You may be expected to contribute towards temple costs – that is the costs incurred by the High Priestess or High Priest of the coven in order to facilitate the meetings. Costs may include everything from incense, candles, flowers and other witchy things – through to practical considerations i.e. tea, coffee, milk, toilet paper etc. Some group leaders will ask the members to provide items which are needed by bringing them along to meetings.

★ Food and Drink for the post ritual feast. This will usually be *"bring and share"* of some description – again it might represent extra expenses, or if you are so inclined you could cook or bake something at a fraction of the cost (and believe us when we say home-baked cakes are always welcome at coven meetings) – but baking does take time, so allow for that if time is an issue!

★ Once you decide that you are able to and willing to commit the time and energy to being in a coven there are further points to consider:

Why do you want to join a coven?
★ Is it a desire to undergo initiation into a particular tradition, the desire to work with others who are likeminded, a desire

to have a teacher that will be able to help you with your development, etc?

★ Are you interested in a particular tradition? There are some traditions, such as the Alexandrian and Gardnerian tradition which are only open to initiates of their tradition, so if one of these (or another initiatory tradition) interested you and you wanted to learn more you would need to join a coven of that tradition.

★ How do you feel about working skyclad (i.e. Naked)? Wiccans from traditions such as the Gardnerian, Alexandrian and derivative traditions practise at least some of their rituals skyclad, some work skyclad only rarely preferring to work robed, whilst others work skyclad on all occasions. How do you feel about being naked with other people of the same and opposite sex? If you have reservations about this, will you be able to overcome it?

★ What are your feelings towards hierarchy? As you should be well aware of by now, Wiccan covens are hierarchical. The High Priestess is the ruler of the coven, a role shared by the High Priest in some groups. Only join a coven if you are willing to listen to instructions and will be able to honour and respect her decisions. Again, the manner in which hierarchy is applied to coveners varies from group to group – so ask for clarification if you are unsure!

Once you have found a group that you are interested in joining you need to be prepared to ask questions to find out as much as you possibly can to ensure that you will be able to comfortably adapt to the way the group works. Each group is going to be unique, although obviously groups from a particular tradition will usually have some things in common. It is worth keeping in mind that you will also be interviewed by the group leaders of the coven you are considering joining. They are likely to give you background information on the group, and will ask questions to determine whether or not you will be suitable for their group. It can take many years to find the 'right' group or you may get lucky and find a group that you can work with pretty much the moment you decide to start looking. What is important is that you may have rejections, – and that at the same time you have the right to also decide that even when you have an offer of membership that you have the right to say no.

Reasons for being turned down for coven membership vary, but remember that it will rarely be personal! Often groups, especially well established groups, will have certain criteria that they test candidates against. For instance, friends of ours have a coven in which they work exclusively with the British Gods. They will only accept members who enjoy working outdoors and have a passion for British Mythology – this is central to their practices and in the nearly ten years we have known them, has never changed. So if you approach them and they asked you about your interests, and you tell them that you have a passion for the Greek and Egyptian Gods and prefer to work indoors, they are obviously unlikely to accept you as a member. Not because you are not good enough, but simply because you don't share in the interests of the group. If you are turned down for membership, ask the group leaders to tell you why they didn't feel you were suitable for their coven. They might be able to give you some tips or point you in the right direction – and if you are lucky they may even be able to refer you to a group that suits your particular interests better.

As emphasised before, every group has their own particular ways of doings things. Every group leader has their own specialities and own life experiences and qualifications, as will every one of the members in such a group- this is what makes each and every group special. Even two groups from the same tradition, following exactly the same rituals will be different, because of the people who are in them. So when you decide to join a group, choose carefully, take your time and it will save you and everyone else involved a lot of heartache and disappointment in the long run.

An established group (regardless of tradition) is unlikely to change for the new person joining - the new person is the one who has to be sure that they will be able to and willing to fit in with the already established group - contributing in time their own efforts and knowledge and life experience to the group in turn, which with time will affect it - which is why a group leader will choose very carefully when allowing someone to join! In addition, it is important to remember that covens are working groups and not just social gatherings.

Pros and cons of working in a coven:
* ★ You will make some of the best friends you will ever have;
* ★ You will have people to share celebration of the Sabbats and your experiences with.
* ★ If you experience problems or need advice you will have a teacher to help you.
* ★ Your training and experience will be paced by the group and its leaders.
* ★ You will have to be committed to being at meetings at specified times.
* ★ You will have to be able to accept criticism and take on board advice at times.
* ★ You become part of an established tradition and are aligned to a specific magickal current (initiatory Wicca).

Further Optional Reading :

* ★ *Inside a Magical Lodge* by John Michael Greer
* ★ *The Real Witches Coven* by Kate West

APPENDIX

1. HOW TO USE INCENSE

In this course you will find some meditations and simple ceremonies that call for the use of incense. Traditionally incense used in Wiccan ceremonies is made by hand using fragrant woods, resins, herbs, oils and flowers. The ingredients are chosen for their magickal properties according to the various energies they correspond with or harmonise with. This type of incense is sometimes called *'loose incense'* or *'grain incense'* to distinguish it from joss sticks and incense cones. In the context of the work you will be doing in this course, you can use loose incense, joss sticks or cones. Fragrant oils burned on an oil burner designed for the purpose may also be used, especially if you suffer from respiratory discomfort or is otherwise asthmatic. Grain incense, when properly prepared by someone skilled in the task and if burned properly, is however definitely the best if you can use it.

Loose incense grains used in the traditional way, are burned on charcoal disks and can be used to fragrance a room, or of course in magickal and devotional ceremonies and other workings. When correctly blended and burned, the grains will release both the fragrances and energies of the herbs and resins blended together into the air. Using incense in this way may be one of the most ancient ways in which the Gods were honoured; it was used in Ancient Sumeria, Egypt, Greece, Rome, India and in many other ancient religious ceremonies.

You will need:
★ Incense Grains
★ Charcoal Discs
★ A heat resistant dish or Censer

Prepare the container in which you will be burning the incense. It is a good idea to place some sand or fine gravel at the bottom of the container to help insulate the censer from the heat and also to allow air to circulate more efficiently around it, which in turn allows it to burn more evenly. (Some censers are designed in a way that this is not necessary)

Light the charcoal disc by holding the edge in a flame (a lighter or candle flame is usually best). If you are worried about burning your fingers, use an old pair of tweezers. Once it ignites you will need to place it in your heat resistant dish and allow it to ignite properly. Sometimes charcoal can be troublesome and you may have to relight it, but with most self-igniting charcoal blocks you should be able to see the sparks travelling across the block. Once the charcoal is fully lit, place approx a ¼ to ½ teaspoon of the incense grains on the block and enjoy! More incense can be added in small quantities as needed.

Useful Suggestions:

★ Incense grains vary according to the ingredients used. If you purchase it *'ready made'* check that only natural ingredients have been used in the blend. Burning synthetic herbs or oils can be very unpleasant!

★ Charcoal blocks burn for approx. 1 hour but this may vary according to both the incense you are burning on it and the flow of air.

★ If you wish to only burn a small amount of incense, you can break a charcoal block in two or even three pieces. It will still be effective, but it may be more difficult to get the grains to stay on top of it!

★ Naturally blended incenses can keep for many years and in most cases improve with age. Keep your incense in a cool, dark place to ensure its longevity!

★ Charcoal disks, once the packet has been opened, absorb moisture from the air and may become difficult to light as a result. Once opened keep them in an airtight container to prevent them from losing their self-igniting properties.

Warnings:

★ If you suffer from any respiratory problems, or are prone to allergies, it is best to avoid the use of incense in enclosed spaces. The smoke may be fragrant and the ingredients natural, but you may still suffer breathing difficulties due to the smoke!

★ Just like with candles, never leave burning incense unattended and keep it away from flammable objects both when you are lighting the charcoal and when it is burning.

★ Occasionally a charcoal block may sparkle profusely upon ignition, so be careful when lighting them!

Supplies (UK)

★ Baldwins – www.baldwins.co.uk
★ Peacock Angel Incense – www.peacockangel.com
★ Star Child (Glastonbury, UK) – www.starchild.co.uk

2. KEEPING YOUR MAGICKAL JOURNAL

One of the most important things to do when you first start practising magick is to create and keep a record of the work you do. This will provide you with a valuable record of your own progress and learning, as well as providing you with a record of what worked best for you. You should preferably keep a handwritten record, some people prefer to keep an electronic record in this day and age, though this has its problems as too often records can get lost due to computer problems! By handwriting your records you will better remember what you are writing about and you will also spend more time thinking about what you are writing, which adds to the learning process.

If you decide to keep your diary electronically consider printing it on a regular basis and keep your records in a file, to ensure that you have a hardcopy of it, should something happen to your computer. If you decide to keep your magickal journal the old fashioned way as a handwritten record we would recommend an A4 or A5 size hardcover notebook. It is worth investing in a larger, rather than smaller notebook, as you will not be limited for space and creative expression as you work through this course. If you prefer you can use a lever arch file, inserting loose sheets of paper and any other material you wish to add as you progress. Using a file has the benefit of providing you with a more flexible system as you will easily be able to add additional material to an earlier section if you decide to do so at a later date. You will also not face the problem of having to remove sheets of paper from a notebook if you make mistakes you want to correct.

The colour, design and type of paper you use are all matters of personal taste, for you to decide on, according to your own personal preferences. It is a good idea to use paper that is easy to write on (especially if you purchase a notebook) as this will make your work a great deal easier!

For each entry you make you should include the following basic information, which may provide you with insights at a later date:

★   The date
★   Phase of the Moon (i.e. Full Moon; Dark Moon, or Full Moon + 3 days; Dark Moon – 5 days; etc)
★   Details of your ritual(s), meditations, or summary of material studied
★   Results (if appropriate) of any workings you did

Women may also want to include details of their menstrual cycles (if appropriate); likewise students who find that the weather affects their moods and sensitivities should also include details of the weather.

Your Magickal Journals are personal and should be treated with care, just like you would do with a personal diary which may contain your innermost secrets and feelings. It is something which should not be shared with others, unless they are trusted friends (or significant others) and also share your interest in magick and in the Wiccan tradition. Details of magickal workings are likewise never discussed outside the magick circle, except in circumstances where you need help or advice with something. In such circumstances, you should speak to someone who you know to be sensitive and understanding to your views and practices, who also have a good level of experience of the subject you are needing help with.

3. THE CHARGE OF THE GODDESS

The *Charge of the Goddess* is a text that has become one of the most important and loved by Wiccans, as well as many other Goddess-centred modern Pagan traditions all over the world. The *Charge of the Goddess* has become a key text towards understanding some of the beliefs of the Wiccan Tradition and as such it is important for any student of Wicca to spend some time reading through and contemplating the concepts therein. It will be referred to throughout this course, so you should keep it to hand to refer to when necessary.

The High Priest kneels and says: "*Listen to the words of the Great Mother, who was of old also called among men, Artemis, Astarte, Dione, Melusine, Aphrodite, Ceridwen, Diana, Arianrhod, Bride, and by many other names...*"

The High Priestess says: "*Whenever ye have need of anything, once in the month, and better it be when the moon is full. Then ye shall assemble in some secret place and adore the spirit of Me who am Queen of all Witcheries. There ye shall assemble, ye who are fain to learn all sorcery, yet who have not won its deepest secrets. To these will I teach things that are yet unknown. And ye shall be free from slavery, and as a sign that ye be really free, ye shall be naked in your rites, and ye shall dance, sing, feast, make music, and love, all in my praise. For mine is the ecstasy of the Spirit, and mine is also joy on earth. For my Law is Love unto all beings. Keep pure your highest ideals. Strive ever towards it. Let naught stop you or turn you aside. For mine is the secret which opens upon the door of youth; and mine is the cup of the Wine of Life: and the Cauldron of Ceridwen, which is the Holy Grail of Immortality. I am the Gracious Goddess who gives the gift of Joy unto the heart of Man. Upon Earth I give the knowledge of the Spirit Eternal, and beyond death I give peace and freedom, and reunion with those who have gone before. Nor do I demand aught in sacrifice, for behold, I am the Mother of all things, and my love is poured out upon earth...*"

The High Priest says: *"Hear ye the words of the Star Goddess, She in the dust of whose feet are the hosts of Heaven, whose body encircleth the universe..."*

The High Priestess continues: *"I who am the beauty of the green earth; and the White Moon amongst the Stars; and the mystery of the Waters; and the desire of the heart of man. I call unto thy soul: arise and come unto me. For I am the Soul of nature who giveth life to the Universe; From me all things proceed; and unto me, all things must return. Beloved of the Gods and men, thine inmost divine self shall be enfolded in the raptures of the infinite. Let my worship be within the heart that rejoiceth, for behold: all acts of love and pleasure are my rituals; and therefore let there be Beauty and Strength, Power and Compassion, Honour and Humility, Mirth and Reverence within you. And thou who thinkest to seek me, know that thy seeking and yearning shall avail thee not unless thou know the mystery, that if that which thou seekest thou findest not within thee, thou wilt never find it without thee, for behold; I have been with thee from the beginning, and I am that which is attained at the end of desire..."*

Note:

This version of the *Charge of the Goddess* is attributed to Doreen Valiente, who was one of Gerald Gardner's High Priestesses during the 1950's. It is believed that she compiled it in 1957. In doing so she drew from a number of published sources, including *"Aradia, Gospel of the Witches"* by Charles G. Leland and from *"The Book of the Law"*, *"The Gnostic Mass"* & *"The Law of Liberty"* by the Victorian magickian Aleister Crowley.

4. TREE MEDITATION

The exercise that follows can be used to create a simple, yet effective sacred space. It is also good for balancing your energy and the energy of the space you find yourself in. Please read through it now, you will be asked to refer back to it in due time as you work through the lessons in this course.

The Tree – A Balancing Exercise & Meditation

It is best to sit or stand for this exercise, which may be performed indoors or outdoors. Start by making yourself comfortable, removing any distractions. First do some gentle stretching exercises, nothing formal, just some movement to ensure that you will be comfortable and aware of your body prior to starting the meditation. If you are wearing shoes and it is practical to do so, remove them.

Close your eyes and take a few deep breaths, allow your body to relax and feel any stresses from your everyday life drain out of you. Inhale and exhale deeply and slowly and then when you feel ready start the following visualisation exercise that will enable you to both balance your energies and create a sacred space around you.

Feel your body becoming heavy as it becomes the trunk of a large tree, visualise branches growing forth from your arms and sprouting from your shoulders and head. See and feel the texture of the bark on the trunk, the different textures on your branches and see leaves, their colour and texture. Next start to put forth roots into the earth from you feet, feel them going deeper and deeper into the earth, breaking through the different layers of soil, rock and deeper still into small underground streams of water, and pockets of air within the earth.

Keeping your awareness of the moist earth beneath you surrounding your roots, continue to breathe rhythmically, and with every in breath, and draw up the energy of Earth and of Water, the minerals and nutrients and water in the earth. Draw them up through your roots, feeling the energising and stimulating energy rise up into your trunk and spread throughout your branches. Allow the energy to sweep throughout your entire being, creating a circuit of energy as the energy flows back through your trunk and roots.

Take a few deep breaths as you allow the Earth and Water energy to circulate throughout your body and then focus your mind on your branches and leaves, reaching upwards towards the heavens; the clouds, the Sun, the Moon and the Planets, the stars. Feel their energy radiating downwards onto your leaves. With every in breath draw in the energy of the Air and of Fire as the light of the Sun into your leaves, down into your branches and into your trunk, allowing it to circulate downwards into your roots and spreading throughout your entire being as it too creates a circuit of energy flowing through your body. Your whole body is a circuit of the Elemental energies flowing in balance.

Continue drawing in energy, so that with each in breath you draw up Earth and Water energy from the earth, and with every out breath you draw down Air and Fire energy from the heavens. Feel the different Elemental energies meeting at your heart centre, coalescing and being transmuted, empowering you with their energy. Feel the energy building up within you. You are now a balanced focus of the energies of the Elements, of the earth beneath you and the heavens above.

5. CHAKRA WORK

The chakras are subtle energy centres in the body. Although the chakras come from Tantra and Indian practices, they have become widely used in Western systems of magick. The standard system describes seven major chakras, six of which are found up the spinal column from the base to the third eye, with the seventh at the top above the head (the crown chakra). The word chakra means *'wheel'* or *'disk'*, a reference to their perceived motion of spinning like a wheel.

The chakras are normally visualised as spinning disks or as lotus flowers, which are also associated with them. Each chakra spins at its own frequency and responds to a different colour; these colours are often used to visualise the chakras easily. The colours correspond to the rainbow as you move up the body, so the base chakra responds to red, the sacral chakra to orange, the solar plexus to yellow, the heart to green, the throat to blue, the third eye to indigo and the crown to violet. The frequency that each chakra spins at can easily be affected by emotions and experiences. When chakras spin too slowly or too quickly it can be connected with emotional problems and physical problems (illnesses).

Remember that our body, emotions, thoughts and spirit are all interconnected. When one part of us is out of balance other parts can also suffer. This is why it is worth taking care of your emotional and spiritual health as well as your physical health. When all are in harmony, you feel great and can achieve your goals more easily. Keeping your chakras balanced is a good practice to include in your life, as it is helping you maintain a greater harmony in yourself. Although Chakras are not part of the *'traditional'* corpus of material studied in Wicca, work with the chakra energy centres is now widely incorporated into the work of many individuals and covens who work within the tradition. It is also an area of practice which is considered universal and which can easily be adapted for use in any system of spiritual practice. The exercises are simple to learn and are very effective. We would recommend you read through all of them now, to familiarise yourself with them. You will be asked to try then out in the Practical exercises section of Lesson 1 and will be able to use them for both balancing your energy body, raising your subtle energy levels and grounding excess energy when need be.

Chakra Balancing Exercise (1)

This exercise is a simple but potent one which keeps the energy body balanced and whole through regular (preferably daily) practice. It can also be used for energising and ensuring you have clear boundaries, so you are not negatively affected by other people's problems. When you visualise the chakras, see them as a disk of around 10cm diameter, apart from the crown, which should be around 30cm in diameter.

Visualise the base chakra as a disk of spinning red light at the base of your spine, and when you see it clearly, inscribe an upright pentagram of gold light on the disk, vibrating (either silently or aloud) the seed sound for the chakra, RA. Then move to the second chakra and visualise it as a disk of spinning orange light, and when it is clear, inscribe an upright gold pentagram on it, vibrating the seed sound, MA.

Continue up the spine, to the solar plexus chakra, visualising it as a spinning disk of yellow light, and when you see it clearly inscribe an upright gold pentagram on it, vibrating the seed sound, DA. Next move up to the heart chakra, visualising it as a spinning disk of green light, and when it is clear inscribe an upright gold pentagram in it as you vibrate the seed sound SA.

Keep moving up the spine, to the throat chakra, which you should visualise as a spinning disk of bright blue light, and when seen clearly, inscribe an upright gold pentagram on it as you vibrate the seed sound, SE (pronounced SAY). Next move to the brow, and visualise the third eye chakra as a spinning disk of deep indigo light, and when you see it clearly inscribe an upright gold pentagram on it, vibrating the seed sound SO.

Finally visualise the crown chakra as a spinning violet disk above your head, with the bottom of the disk just brushing the top of your head. When you see it clearly, inscribe an upright gold pentagram on it and vibrate the seed sound HUNG. After having inscribed the pentagram on the crown chakra, imagine each pentagram was a seed, and visualise that seed bursting forth gold light, surrounding the body and filling the aura, completely permeating your being, both physical and subtle. When you can feel the gold light surrounding your body, concentrate the energy on any areas of the body which are in pain or feel weaker.

For the best results we suggest doing this on a daily basis. If you include it in your daily routine, it will greatly strengthen your aura. If you work in an environment which is unpleasant or distasteful to you in some manner, try adding an extra piece onto the end of the exercise, where you visualise the outside of your aura like a mirror, reflecting anything negative back to its source.

Chakra Opening & Closing Exercises

The following exercises are for specifically opening and closing your chakras. Before you perform any magickal work, such as meditations, rituals or spells, ensuring your chakras are open enables you to fully experience your own subtle energies and also to interact with the subtle energies in your environment. If you know you are going to be in a situation that could be disturbing or distressing, or around people who always leave you feeling drained, closing your chakras for the duration of this time helps you remain more focused as you are consciously choosing not to allow anything around you to drain any of your energy.

The visualisations involve seeing the chakras in their other form as lotuses. Each chakra lotus has a specific number of petals associated with it, which is included in these exercises, both as the number of petals you see, and as the number of times you vibrate the mantra. These exercises are slightly more complex than the previous exercise, but easy once you get going, and well worth learning.

Chakra Opening Exercise (2)

For this exercise, you visualise the chakras like flower buds which are slightly open. As the chakras are never fully closed, unless you feel the need to be completely detached from your environment, their usual state is a degree of openness. The degree of openness will depend on your way of dealing with the world.

See your base chakra as a slightly open red flower bud, opening its four petals as you vibrate the mantra RA four times. Feel the energy start to rise up your spine, see it golden in colour, rising up to your sacral chakra, which you see as an orange flower. See it open its six orange petals as you vibrate the mantra MA six times.

Be aware of the golden energy continuing to ascend your spine, to your solar plexus chakra. See the ten yellow petals of the solar plexus chakra open as you vibrate the mantra DA ten times. See the golden energy continue its ascent up your spine to your heart chakra. See the twelve green petals of the heart chakra open as you vibrate the mantra SA twelve times. From here feel the golden energy rise to your throat chakra, and see it open its sixteen blue petals as you vibrate the mantra SE sixteen times.

From the throat, see the golden energy rise up to your brow, to your third eye chakra. See the two indigo petals of the third eye chakra open as you vibrate the mantra SO twice. Then see the golden energy rise up to the crown of your head, and see the thousand violet petals of the crown chakra open as you vibrate the mantra HUNG fifty times. (Although there are a thousand petals, it would take a very long time to recite the mantra a thousand times, and fifty is also a number of completion like one thousand, representing the fifty petals of the six major chakras from the base to the third eye).

Chakra Closing Exercise (3)

To close the chakras, you basically perform the reverse of the previous opening exercise. Note that when you see the chakra petals closing, they do not close completely but to a slightly open state, so you can still interact with the energies of your environment and other people.

See your crown chakra as an open thousand-petalled violet flower, and vibrate the mantra HUNG fifty times as you see the petals closing to a slightly open bud state.

Move down to your third eye chakra, seeing it as an open two-petalled indigo flower, and see the petals closing to the slightly open bud state as you vibrate the mantra SO twice.

Keep moving down to your throat chakra, seeing it as an open sixteen-petalled blue flower. Visualise the petals closing to the slightly open state as you vibrate the mantra SE sixteen times.

Next move down your spine to the heart chakra, seeing it as an open twelve petalled green flower. Visualise the petals closing to the slightly open bud state as you vibrate the mantra SA twelve times.

Continue down to your solar plexus chakra, seeing it as an open ten-petalled yellow flower. Visualise the petals closing to the slightly open bud state as you vibrate the mantra DA ten times.

Continuing down, see the sacral chakra as an open six-petalled orange flower. Visualise the petals closing to the slightly open bud state as you vibrate the mantra MA six times.

Next move down to the base chakra, seeing it as an open four petalled red flower. Visualise the petals closing to the slightly open bud state as you vibrate the mantra RA four times.

Other books by this author:

If you enjoyed this book you may also find the following books by the author Sorita d'Este of interest:

<u>Practical Magick, Meditation & Ceremony</u>
Wicca Magickal Beginnings
Circle of Fire
Practical Elemental Magick
Practical Planetary Magick
Avalonia's Book of Chakras

<u>History, Mythology & Folklore</u>
The Isles of the Many Gods
The Guises of the Morrigan
Artemis: Virgin Goddess of the Sun & Moon

<u>Anthologies (Edited by Sorita d'Este)</u>
Horns of Power
Hekate: Keys to the Crossroads
Priestesses, Pythonesses & Sybils

These books and many more are available from all good esoteric bookstores, as well as directly from: **www.avaloniabooks.co.uk**

Biographies

About the Author : Sorita d'Este

Author and esoteric researcher Sorita d'Este describes herself as a student of life's little mysteries. She is passionate about the western traditions of magick and mysticism, her interests and work span a wide range of subjects including the Celtic, Greek and Egyptian traditions, medieval and renaissance grimoires and palmistry. Her published works include such titles as *Practical Planetary Magick*; *Practical Elementary Magick*; *Circle of Fire*; *Wicca Magickal Beginnings*; and *The Isles of the Many Gods*, which she co-wrote with her husband David Rankine. She also edited the anthologies *Hekate: Keys to the Crossroads* and *Horns of Power: Manifestations of the Horned God*. Sorita has lectured extensively on folklore, mythology and magick; and she is the co-founder of the *StarStone Network*. She lives in Monmouthshire with her husband David Rankine and their son. To find out more about her work visit: **www.avalonia.co.uk**

About the Artist: Emily Carding

The cover of *Towards the Wiccan Circle* is graced by *Blodeuwedd*, a painting of this Welsh flower Goddess who is transformed into an owl. It was painted by the artist Emily Carding, a visionary artist who lives in a tiny village in rural East Sussex (England), with her true love and a beautiful little girl. Emily is a priestess and a Reiki master and has been using and studying Tarot since 1994. She practices Celtic Shamanism, studying with John and Caitlin Matthews and with her partner Julian Clark, with whom she is working through the Merlin's Wisdom series of initiatory gateways. Since focusing on a career in art she has been published widely, including the *We'moon date book*, *The Tarot Lover's Calendar*, regular appearances in *Pentacle Magazine*, and a small press limited edition of the Major Arcana of her first deck, *The Tarot of the Sidhe*, published by Adam McLean. Her first major publication, the *Transparent Tarot*, is due to be released by *Schiffer Books* in October 2008.

To find out more about her work visit: **www.childofavalon.com**

Lightning Source UK Ltd.
Milton Keynes UK

176386UK00001B/22/P